SOME MODERN POETS

SOME
MODERN POETS

AND OTHER
CRITICAL ESSAYS

BY

EDWARD DAVISON

Essay Index Reprint Series

BOOKS FOR LIBRARIES PRESS
FREEPORT, NEW YORK

LIBRARY OF CONGRESS CATALOG CARD NUMBER:

68-16926

PRINTED IN THE UNITED STATES OF AMERICA

TO
L. H. W. AND J. S. W.

ACKNOWLEDGMENT

Certain of these essays appeared originally in *The London Mercury, The Fortnightly Review, The English Journal, The Saturday Review of Literature,* and *The Reader,* to whose editors I am indebted.

E. D.

CONTENTS

A WORD FOR TRADITION

A Word for Tradition

THE chief traditions of English poetry may be reduced from a thousand details, very broadly and briefly, to a few general statements. Recapitulation cannot be without value at a time when *a priori* ideas concerning literature are becoming as common as books of worthless verse. Not to beg the question "What Is Poetry?" with some theoretical definition, it may be said, in the phrase of Sir Arthur Quiller-Couch, that it is the "kind of thing that the poets have written." It appears, taking this kind of thing all in all, at its best, that the poets whose names we honour have accepted and passed on certain guiding traditions. The poet writes in patterns of verse, either already existing or, maybe, self-invented. These are governed variously by repetitions of rhythm (and, sometimes, also of rhyme), admitting such variations as can be achieved without offending the essential character of the basic pattern. The musical result can only be judged by the degree of pleasure attending both the

3

fulfilment and unfulfilment of the reader's ex-
pectations which the pattern itself has created.
Neither fulfilment nor unfulfilment should
create displeasure. Any subject is fit for poetry
if it has been felt in the right way. This in-
volves the poet's emotional, and, sometimes, his
intellectual integrity; but it does not involve accepted ideas of truth or untruth. There is also
a tradition that poetry should be generally intel-
ligible. The poet can borrow anything he
likes from the works of other writers and is
justified in doing so in every instance where
he improves or has obviously attempted to improve his original. A comprehensive view of
the "kind of thing the poets have written" also
reveals that, in all ages and countries, poets
have been particularly interested in certain phenomena of human existence, such problems and
feelings as surround, for instance, the perennial
occurrence of birth, death, love, in its various
aspects, the changes wrought by time, and in
some obvious concrete evidences and symbols
of these occurrences, as children, stars, flowers,

mountains, graves, and so forth. On or around
such themes great poems have been written in
every age. Very justly we say of such poems
that they treat traditional subjects.

There are no rules for the writing of poetry,
only these few guiding traditions which it is in
the power of any good poet to modify or increase. The current tendency is to view new
poems wherein these traditions are observed as
if they were merely academic exercises. Many
critics approach them in a spirit that seems to
suggest that the poets of the past had a mo-
nopoly of genuine feeling in their attitudes
toward the perennial subjects of poetry. They
do so in contempt of the fact that recent poetry,
in many fine instances, has confirmed the existence of these traditional interests in the twentieth century no less than in the fifth century
B. C. Mr. Gordon Bottomley's "Atlantis,"
and Flecker's "To a Poet a Thousand Years
Hence" may be particularly recalled. In the
latter

> I care not if you bridge the seas
>   Or ride secure the cruel sky,

5

Or build consummate palaces
Of metal or of masonry.

But have you wine and music still
    And statues, and a bright-eyed love,
And foolish thoughts of good and ill,
    And prayers to those who sit above?

How shall we conquer? Like a wind
    That blows at eve our fancies blow;
And old Maeonides the Blind
    Said it three thousand years ago.

Mr. A. E. Housman has the seed of the whole realization in his poem "On Wenlock Edge," not to mention a score of others in his two little books. The Shropshire Lad looks at the heaving Wrekin near the ruins of the Uriconum, the old Roman city, realizing that

. . . . before my time, the Roman
At yonder heaving hill would stare:
The blood that warms an English yeoman,
The thoughts that hurt him, they were there,

There, like the wind through woods in riot,
Through him the gale of life blew high;

6

A WORD FOR TRADITION

The tree of man was never quiet:
Then 'twas the Roman, now 'tis I.

The gale, it plies the saplings double,
It blows so hard, 'twill soon be gone:
Today the Roman and his trouble
Are ashes under Uricon.

It is not easy to know why the current critical
attitude towards the traditions embodied in such
poetry as this should so often be false and un-
friendly. A young poet beginning at the present time to express his peculiar temperamental
response to the perennial sources of wonder, on
lines traditionally parallel to those followed by
his great predecessors, is compelled to run a
worse gauntlet than any that is awaiting the
poet who ignores the ancient materials. Only
the rarest kind of critical faculty is able to distinguish infallibly between the kind of verse
where a mere imitator employs the traditional
materials in traditional verse and, on the other
hand, such poetry as has been honestly conceived and written in the traditional spirit. It
does not, of course, require any very great in-

7

sight to recognize the difference between the traditional extremes of Mr. Robert Bridges and Mr. Edgar A. Guest. But unless that insight is accompanied by a realization that the difference is one not merely of quality, but also of kind, the critic might as well be without it.

In various epochs the traditions of English poetry have been whittled down by temporary conventions, customs and rules artificially imposed by a passing generation. The epochs when men have prolonged their offenses against the traditions have inevitably been succeeded by epochs of literary revolt. New poets insist upon the destruction of the hampering conventions and restore the permanent traditions. Wordsworth and Coleridge, for instance, attacked and defeated some powerful conventions that had restricted and staled the form, language, and range of English poetry for nearly a hundred years. They were not, as is often supposed, the enemies of tradition. A good poet is bound to be a rebel against convention unless he can forge it to his uses in such a way as to bring it under the rule of the traditions.

8

Thus Shakespeare mastered the conventions of the Elizabethan love-sonnet which, in many contemporary hands, had offended the tradition of poetic integrity. He converted a form of superior *vers de société* into the living sonnets we know. He destroyed a convention to create a tradition. Milton destroyed a convention that had made rhyme an almost inseparable part of poetry, and created, within the poetic tradition which he restored, a tradition of Miltonic blank verse. In our own time Mr. Vachel Lindsay split a lance against the convention of verse-written-to-be-read and, in some quarters, restored a very ancient tradition of verse-written-to-be-declaimed. Any tradition which excludes other traditions is one which is in danger of becoming a convention. The convention that led the poets of a bygone age to say in heroic couplets anything and everything they had to say offended the tradition in just the same way as the gradually dying modern convention whereby many poets persisted in saying their all in free verse. Poetry is inseparable from its traditions. But we live now in an

9

age so inured to the idea of "revolt" in poetry
that amid the continual flux of reactions and
counter-reactions, little attempt is made to distinguish the rebel against tradition from the
rebel against convention. Who knows what our
own conventions are?

A celebrated contemporary historian has un-
ashamedly declared that "Tradition is the
bread-and-butter of civilization." He is in no
way belied because the platitude must have been
hoary when men built the Parthenon. But, because so many of our half-wits retreat to its
convenient shelter when their opinions are
called into court, there is no need to jib at the
reiteration of a truth which the history of civilization, no less than of literature, the "fine
flower of civilization," confirms in every chapter. The literary critic neglects such platitudes
at his own peril. Today when the word traditional is applied to poetry, as often as not, as a
derogatory epithet, it is only too easy to forget
that a poet may, and often does, follow the
oldest traditions of his art and yet merit the
highest admiration. Mr. Robert Bridges, the

10

English poet-laureate, perhaps the most traditional of all living poets, is nevertheless ranked, at least by his fellow-artists, among the best lyric and narrative poets of our times. In America, Mr. Robert Frost and Mr. E. A. Robinson, both traditional poets (if the word has any meaning at all), are now generally considered, after years of neglect, as the chief exponents of their art. The achievement of all three poets reveals a greater freedom and more extensive range than one remembers to have observed in the work of the self-declared "revolutionary" poets who have attempted to forswear the traditions during the past two decades.

It is time then, risking platitudes, to insist that new poetry of the traditional order should be approached on its merits and not in the unreasonably suspicious and timid spirit now increasingly revealed by so many of those journeymen critics and reviewers whose responsibility it is to introduce an author to his immediate audience. It is imperative to recognize that "poetry is a continuous movement." Poetry has always begotten poetry. Shakespeare, of all poets the most original, was also the most imitative. Keats acknowledges a score of debts, notably to Spenser, Milton, and Dryden. Shelley, in many of his finest passages, derives from Aeschylus and Shakespeare. And Mr. John Masefield would not be the poet he is if Chaucer had never written "The Canterbury Tales." Poetry will continue to beget poetry in the old way. The absence of such influences in the work of a beginning poet, or even of a mature poet, is seldom a sign of virtue.

But criticism today, especially that hand-to-mouth criticism, reviewing, which is more generally read and certainly more influential at present than more reputable essays in literary appreciation, is degraded by the prevalence of several fallacious *a priori* notions concerning poetry and the influence of poets on one another. None is so dangerously misleading, so unjustifiably preconceived, as the muddled notion that a regard for poetic traditions is incompatible with poetic individuality. There is a general tendency to interpret as synonymous the terms "traditional" and "conventional," on one hand, and "derivative" and "imitative," on the other. The old procedure of reviewers has been turned topsy-turvy since the days when Jeffrey and Gifford damned a new poet if he failed to write in some recognized mode. It is not uncommon for their living successors to deny virtue to new poetry for no better reason than that it does follow a recognized mode. Needless to say one extreme is as bad as the other. In both instances the critic declines to take poetry as it is written, for what it is (not for what it claims to be), and to judge it on its particular merits or demerits. Apart from the consideration of such extremes, it appears—and any representative collection of current reviews will illustrate the convention—that good poetry of the traditional kind (excluding, of course, the work of established poets like Mr. E. A. Robinson or Mr. A. E. Housman) is treated unfairly and ungenerously in comparison with meritorious work that is not in the broad tradition. Thus poets as remarkable as Mr. George Santayana or Mr. Robert Nichols do not receive the same amount of contemporary critical attention as, say, Mr. E. E. Cummings or Mr. T. S. Eliot. Such a state of affairs is absurd and cries for remedy quite apart from the particular merits of the various poets concerned.

The existing prejudice—for it deserves no kinder description—against traditional poetry can, of course, be explained as a very natural reaction against the past age of conservative literary authority. One kind of intolerance and narrow-mindedness has been substituted for another. But a twentieth-century quarrel, like that of Crites and his friends in Dryden's "Essay," between the "ancients" of the day-before-yesterday and the "moderns" of the day-after-tomorrow, can only be unprofitably ridiculous. There have been many attempts to provoke such a quarrel during the past fifteen years. Some of our self-styled "rebels" have frightened the journeymen critics (and not a small number of editors) into the ignorant and cowardly attitude that turns its back upon many facts and questions concerning the value of tradition in poetry.

14

A typical instance could have been noticed recently in the prospectus of a new "advanced" magazine originating in New York. It was declared unequivocally that the editors would not print any poems concerning moonlight and roses. The magazine was planned to represent the art and interests of "The Age of the Machine." There was no reason to suppose that the declaration was not to be taken quite literally. One might travel far without finding a better experiment in the ancient art of cutting off one's nose to spite one's face. Admittedly, roses and moonlight have been responsible for as much bad verse, throughout the ages, as any other phenomena of the physical world. But to think of poetry in terms of "subjects" is to misapprehend its essential nature. It is the nature of a poet's feeling about his "subject" that is important, not the subject itself. English poetry robbed of its moonlight and roses would be the poorer by scores of its loveliest pages. An editor, setting out to glorify a machine age, is not, of course, compelled to print such excellent poems, and passages from

15

poems, as have actually been written about moonlight and roses by living poets like Mr. Walter de la Mare, Mr. Robert Frost, Mr. W. B. Yeats, Mr. John Freeman, and Mr. W. H. Davies, to name only a few whose work immediately occurs to mind. But a predetermined refusal of such poems appears, in the end, as a refusal to recognize that poets in a machine age actually do write good poems about moonlight and roses. We are opposed not to a reasonable view of poetry so much as to a mere reactionary prejudice against certain physical objects which may or may not be the immediate causes of excellent poetry. It need not be denied that an automobile, or any other machine, is potentially as worthy and likely a subject for poetry, especially today, as the reddest roses that ever faded in a moonlit garden. But is a good poem about a machine necessarily better than a good poem about a rose? And shall we add anything worth having to literature by persuading the poetasters to give up their moonlight and roses in favor of electric fans and typewriting machines? It would be more profitable to recall Mr. Laurence Binyon's "Invocation to Youth."

> Come then, as ever, like the wind at morning!
>   Joyous, O Youth, in the aged world renew
> Freshness to feel the eternities around it,
>   Rain, stars and clouds, light and the sacred dew.
>   The strong sun shines above thee:
>   That strength, that radiance bring!
>   If Winter come to Winter,
>   When shall men hope for Spring?

Criticism apparently too easily forgets that although one poet may be writing, like Mr. Carl Sandburg, about the time of the machine, another forgets it completely in contemplating time itself. Thus Mr. Robert Nichols, a poet by no means unaware of the century in which he lives, nevertheless surpasses himself and most of the rebels in a lyric that might have been written to answer Mr. Binyon's invocation.

Alone on the shore in the pause of the night-time
I stand, and I hear the long wind blow light;
I view the constellations quietly, quietly burning;
I hear the wave fall in the hush of the night.

Long after I am dead, ended this bitter journey,
Many another whose heart holds no light
Shall your solemn sweetness hush, awe, and comfort,
O my companions, Wind, Waters, Stars and Night.

I have usually found that those who insist loudest that the modern poet should take care to reflect the particular life and thought of his own generation are the same people who object most noisily to dead poets (Tennyson, for instance) who were at pains to do the same thing for their own age.

It may be granted that most of our "advanced" poets and critics are not merely playing up to a deliberate "stunt," that they are, at least, emotionally honest. But most who have declared themselves the enemies of the so-called "wornout traditions" can usually be shown to be victims of some prejudice of the kinds suggested above. Since the "Imagists" issued their manifesto some thirteen years ago,—a manifesto containing such demonstrably false preconceptions of the poetic art that one marvels now that anybody took pains to prove them so at the time,—since then, the "new" poets, as well as the critics and reviewers who have acclaimed them, have been lamentably backward in stating any kind of credo which could survive critical examination. In the absence of some critical attitude formulated in applied opposition to (what should be) the easily anticipated objections of their opponents, it is not unjust to assume the existence of some prejudice based on feelings of mere reaction. For wise and reasonable reaction is inevitably governed by ideas that can be formulated in organized detail. But we may search almost in vain for such criticism. Indeed, the only recent poet whose revolutionary theories appear to have a basis tenable in terms of reasoned literary criticism is Mr. T. S. Eliot. And even he required the careful apologetics of that brilliant psychologist and critic, Mr. I. A. Richards, before it was possible to come to intellectual grips with the *raison d'être* of his poetry.

Perhaps the only way to account for the failures and prejudices discussed in this essay is to recognize the fact that we are all too self-conscious in our views of the position this age will occupy in history. We are, moreover, too much interested in the future of literature to pay a proportionate regard to its past. When Mr. Christopher Morley wrote from England "Leave the future of American literature to take care of itself" his voice was crying against the wind. It would never be heard by the countless authors and reviewers who live on the *qui vive*, anxious to be among those who will first hail the appearance of another Whitman, a Californian Keats, or a Manhattan Balzac. Like the public for which they make their promises and prophecies they are living on their literary nerves. Such an attitude might easily involve self-defeat when the great moment comes. The next chapter in the history of literature will not necessarily be unlike all those that preceded it. And even if, in the end, it appears that we have been entertaining angels unawares, there is not yet any good reason to suppose that those angels will necessarily be the authors who have turned their backs against the traditions upon which poetry has thrived since the days of Shakespeare.

20

ANALYZED RHYME

Frank Kendon and Analyzed Rhyme

NEARLY four years ago, in England, a young and unknown poet published his first experiment in Analyzed Rhyme. The lyric "I Spend My Days Vainly" (from *Poems by Four Authors*, Bowes & Bowes, Cambridge, England, 1923) passed without any comment upon its peculiar and original rhyme construction although it was actually quoted and praised by nine out of ten reviewers. In a note appended to a later volume of his verse, Mr. Frank Kendon invited the attention of his readers to the device; but scarcely a leaf stirred in the critical wilderness. There could be no more pregnant comment on the integrity of the people who, for ten years, had been crying in England for some innovation that might extend the capacities of the poetic instrument. No one of them realized that Mr. Kendon had added to it a completely new string. Perhaps in America where the same kind of anxiety expressed itself recently in quarrels and controversies over "Polyphonic Prose,"—that dead ass of John

23

Lyly flogged into some semblance of life by Miss Lowell,—perhaps here some poets and critics may be found to interest themselves in one of the most remarkable inventions any living poet has presented to his fellow artists. With very few exceptions, critics and reviewers alike, on both sides of the Atlantic (less blameworthily in America because Mr. Kendon's *Poems and Sonnets* [John Lane, 1924] has been available only in the English edition) have ignored it. Mr. Louis Untermeyer alluded to it briefly in a note in his anthology of English poets, but did not appear to recognize its extraordinary character. Thus, until the writing of this present belated advertisement, little more than a few unregarded whispers have been uttered concerning Analyzed Rhyme.

It is not, perhaps, merely the exaggeration of a would-be prophet to say that the publication of Mr. Frank Kendon's *Poems and Sonnets* will ultimately be held to mark an epoch-making addition to the history of poetic technique. That his invention is a technical one need not subtract from the interest of the layman. The time

24

has long since passed when argument about the material of poetry could be profitably undertaken. Criticism today devotes itself—or ought to devote itself—to two chief considerations: the one, value; the other, ways and means (*i.e.*, the technique) of the artist. In this essay we are not primarily concerned with the value of Mr. Kendon's poetry, but rather with the validity and consequences of his new approach to rhyme. Let the quality of his poetry speak for itself in such brief quotations as shall follow.

Critics and poets, whatever shade of opinion they represent, are doubtless agreed that any addition to the mechanics of verse which will permit a larger range of artistic expression than lies within the capability of existing means is to be warmly welcomed. Rhyme has been alternately praised and abused as a technical device in the art of versification. Every school ·boy knows Milton's opinions on the subject, although a larger number of commentators (not all of them schoolboys) do not appear to know that his "attack" on rhyme was directed particularly against its conventional use, at the time, as the vehicle for heroic poetry. Thus, very frequently, when the validity of rhyme is questioned, Milton's name is quoted in support of views which he, the author of "Lycidas" and "Il Penseroso," would certainly have repudiated with lashing contempt.

Most of the old arguments against rhyme no longer concern us. The chief remaining objection—that rhyme is "a troublesome modern bondage"—rests on two principal contentions. The first tells us that a poet is compelled to tamper with his spontaneous thoughts and impulses in order to serve the requirements of rhyme. Thus, it is said, he undermines his own integrity. This view has already been contradicted very effectively by the author of that fine book, *Convention and Revolt in Poetry*, Mr. J. L. Lowes. It need not detain us here except while we insist that every requirement of artistic expression tends equally to prevent spontaneity. How very easy it is to forget that poetry is an art and not a physical act, like blowing one's nose or taking off one's trousers. Thus, from time to time, the camp followers of literature tend to disregard all that careful moulding and welding, that highly conscious craftsmanship which is carried on so continually behind the poetic scenes. A few hours with any good collection of manuscript poems by the great masters will suffice to upset most popular ideas about that contradiction in terms, "unpremeditated art." To the poet in the act of composition every possible method, every rhyme, every "trick" of word-craft is a welcome, potential means of self-expression. But to most people attempting poetry each new requirement of reason, rhythm and rhyme is an additional obstacle, a hindrance to, not a means of, expression. Rhyme has been and remains a valuable means to certain poetic ends. Those who would cast it off are merely attempting to relieve such practitioners of verse as cannot, in the face of technical difficulties, help themselves. They are, moreover, usually such as conceive rhyme as a mere decoration of verse and not, as it always has been in skilful hands, a powerful poetic force.

27

The second and, hitherto, more tenable contention insists that rhyme in the English language has lost its ancient bloom, that its flowers have been withered and staled by constant exposure to the gentle reader. English is admittedly less rich in rhymes than some rival languages. There is an inevitable tendency for certain words to pair off again and again in rhyme,—moon with soon, love with above, or prove, and so forth through a thousand instances. Constant repetition has wrung the sap out of many such rhymes. So runs the argument.

Where'-e'er you find "the cooling western breeze,"
In the next line, it "whispers through the trees:"
If crystal streams "with pleasing murmur creep,"
The reader's threatened (not in vain) with "sleep."

Where Pope blamed the poet the advocates of this view blame the language. Push their contention to its logical conclusion and it breaks down. For if the virtue really has departed from such rhymes, why has it not also departed from the poems (or passages) by Shakespeare,

28

Chaucer, Keats, and Wordsworth wherein the rhymes appear? Perhaps the fault does lie in the poet after all. Nevertheless, it is impossible not to admit some degree of justice in this complaint. The English language has, from the outset, limited certain words to a very small number of alternative rhymes. Some words, like "month," have no reasonable rhymes at all. Excepting in the hands of the most skilful and conscientious artists in verse, rhyming does remain either too difficult on the one hand, or too easy on the other; either way a constant snare for the unwary writer. It is also true that quite a large number of rhymes do present themselves as jaded, even when they are well and effectively employed, though none so stale that it cannot, in master hands, be thoroughly revivified. (It is perhaps not unfair to suggest that the best rhyming is always the least noticeable, as in the later work of Mr. W. B. Yeats and such a poem as Mr. Robert Frost's "A Time to Talk.") The "revolutionary" cure for this not very serious disease has been, of course, to abandon rhyme almost completely. Such a course, however, is much too careless and easy. Poetry has been left the poorer by the loss of all those graces it would borrow from rhyme. Not for the first time the baby has been thrown out with the bath.

Nothing in the foregoing remarks is to be taken as a belittlement of the various very real inconveniences attending on the use (or misuse) of rhyme. No man who has written a mere half dozen of sonnets can doubt the reality of those inconveniences. The suggestion is that the dissatisfied sonneteer blame his artistry rather than the English language. To reject rhyme altogether is a sulky evasion, not a solution. Ninety per cent of our alleged revolutionary movements in literature and art today can be described with equal truth as sulky evasions. Let no one be deceived by the noise that generally disguises the sulkiness. Let us recollect that the great changes in literature have been wrought very quietly by quiet men. Cervantes beat no big drum; no man yet made less commotion in his immediate passage through this world than William Shakespeare;

even those nonconformists, Coleridge and Wordsworth, whose freedom we inherit, were never noisy in their nonconformity. All four men together made less fuss about their problems in art than, in our own time, we have heard from the Imagists alone. *Mais où sont les neiges d'antan!* Mr. Kendon has made no noise at all. The purpose of the remaining part of this essay, now that the ground has been more or less cleared, is to make some little noise for him, or, rather, perhaps, for his solution of these various difficulties concerning the nature and use of rhyme.

The complaints already reviewed can now be stated fairly simply in terms of a regret, many times expressed by English poets; a regret that a language rich in all other respects does not offer a larger and therefore more manageable variety of admissible rhymes. Attempts have been made, time without number, to substitute some kind of half-rhyme, assonance or echo in the place of true rhyme, seldom with any distinguished success. Thus in "Strange Meet-

31

ing" Wilfred Owen, evading the inevitable
familiarities of rhyme, writes—

> . . . by my glee might many men have laughed,
> And of my weeping something has been left,
> Which must die now. I mean the truth untold,
> The pity of war, the pity war distilled.
> Now men will go content with what we spoiled,
> Or, discontent, boil bloody and be spilled,
> They will be swift with swiftness of the tigress.
> None will break ranks, though nations trek from
>   progress.

But although this is one of Owen's finest poems,
surely it is successful in spite of rather than by
means of the false rhymes. It might of course
be maintained that their dissonance contributes
something to the hasty, tender pity of the
thought, that it has a kind of contrapuntal effect
that harmonizes with the sense. How are such
delicacies to be measured? Nevertheless, dissonance or assonance, the rhymes are false
rhymes, no-rhymes, not even half-rhymes like
cup, crop; home, come; drive, live; love, prove
—wherein the vowels are all but twinned, and

only a deliberately perverted ear would pretend that they gain an effect in the least similar to the effect of true rhyme. Instances of such false rhyming might easily be multiplied in contexts bad as well as good. It would always, I think, be found that they lack that essential quality which is present in true rhyme.

Mr. Kendon's very simple invention, however, is open to no such objection as both eye and ear might justifiably urge against Owen for laugh and left, untold and distilled. He resolves such discords. Instead of seeking for something essentially different from true rhyme he has utilized all the elements it contains and yet achieved a completely new grouping of words on a basis of their common sound. The chief difference between common rhyme and analyzed rhyme is that words are ranked not in pairs, but in sets of four. The method is actually much simpler than it sounds. Simple rhyme consists of an exact echo of the last vowel and consonantal sounds of a word, as in soon, moon; hide, pride. Mr. Kendon takes two such

33

words as soon and hide, but separates the vowel from the consonantal sounds before looking for his rhymes. The "*oo*" of soon is united with the *d* of hide; and the *i* of hide with the *n* of soon. This simple analysis produces the rhyming sounds

oon	ine
ide	ood

as a basis for new sets of words. Thus, by means of analyzed rhyme, an absolute sound relationship can be established between words that have hitherto seemed alien to each other. Here are some examples:

soon	brine
hide	food
moon	divine
bride	pursued

A few other random examples employing different sounds may also be given.

love	won
seen	grieve

34

ANALYZED RHYME

month	plinth
fling	sung
see	sheen
dawn	awe
height	float
whole	style
hate	Detroit
spoil	scale

More elaborate examples with double endings appear later. Mr. Kendon's own exposition must be quoted.

A true rhyming termination [says Mr. Kendon] is generally made up of vowel and consonant. "Analyzed Rhyme" takes notice of both elements, as true rhyme does, but splits the endings up and interchanges the vowels. Thus—

I spend my days vainly
    Not in delight;
Though the world is elate,
    And tastes her joys finely.

Here wrapped in slow musing
  Lies my dark mind,
To no music attuned
  Save its own, and despising

The lark for remoteness,
  The thrush for bold lying,
The soft wind for blowing,
  And the round sun for brightness.

O tarry for me, sweet;
  I shall stir, I shall wake!
And the melody you seek
  Shall be lovely, though late!

vainly and elate have rhyming vowels and
different consonants, so have delight and
finely; while vainly and finely have rhyming consonantal endings and different vowels, and so have delight and elate. This,
though it rather increases the bondage,
which is no real disadvantage, provides an
entirely new set of pairs.

Mr. Kendon proceeds to call attention to one
of the sonnets in his book in which the new

method is used in conjunction with ordinary
rhyme.

> I think, if I had alchemy enough,
> Earth's vernal sweetness, that intoxicates
> My body and my spirit, would lie safe
> In words at last. But when the couplet shuts
> Its final rhyme upon this sonnet, I,
> With weary mind perusing, shall not find
> Much magic reminiscent of the sky,
> Nor breathe again the blossom-loaded wind.

A similar and perhaps more elaborate mixture
of the two methods appears in the following
fragment by another poet who has experimented
with Mr. Kendon's invention.

Because of trees he left the fields behind,
Left his fresh horses at the tilted plough
In the mid-furrow, and forgot to bar the gate;
  The hamlet he passed by,
And his own tidy plot of garden ground
He passed, without a glance, before the sun
Uplit the clouds, striding like one elate
Who goes to keep some tryst in Avalon.

37

And all the way he watched the streamers ride
In purple and red with one faint flag of green
Above the tents of dawn where many a lark uprose
     Singing, nor stayed his speed
Uphill, but plunged into the farther chine,
And ran down lightly to the river-meadows;
For there the sunlight suddenly overflows
The misty East and scatters all the shadows.

Then at the bridge he lingered. Not so long
As a bee takes to taste a water-lily
He gazed on three bare willows crouch't beside the
    stream,
     And knew his heart unwilling
To leave them in their natural melancholy.
For that he sighs: though woods unvisited
Await him, he half-quenches an old dream
Of a drowned girl with willows garlanded.

Therefore he takes his knife and clambers down
To trim the ragged osiers where they trail
Among the drifting weeds, and one decaying bough
     He chops away—in vain!
Already the dark cancer veins befoul
The pith within the shoulder, and the tree

Must die and rot; he cannot save it now.
Better to take his road and let it be.

But the most effective of all Mr. Kendon's examples is his lovely lyric "From this fair
night"—

From this fair night to draw sweet music down
A long-benighted wind makes harps of trees,
And, not to lose the sight while men's eyes drowse,
The moon gives light and stares upon the scene.

Dew upon dew condenses; from the city
Chimes of far-away bells the hours attune,
The silver landscape, no man walks wherein,
Unto itself is sweet, a secret beauty.

Oh that content, content might softly so
Steal over me and cheat this longing for fame,
That I might love the trees about my home,
Or well enough sing to throw the songs away.

Mr. Kendon is, I think, a little over-cautious
in saying that "it would be foolish to claim that
the effect is exactly the same as that of rhyme."
I have personally read these poems to various
people, including several well-known poets,

who did not notice the difference (especially in verses which employed feminine endings) until it was actually called to their attention. But the truth of Mr. Kendon's suggestion that "this is a new and more subtle tune in words," has, I think, been amply demonstrated by his practice. Analyzed Rhyme has not yet been attempted, so far as I know, by anybody except the inventor and one or two of his personal friends in England. This is not, I think, due to disinterest so much as to ignorance. Most of the poets who would probably be attracted by the opportunity to experiment with this fascinating form have never heard of it. A time will come when they or their successors will.

ROBERT BURNS

SOME RECONSIDERATIONS

Robert Burns

Some Reconsiderations

ROBERT BURNS died in 1797, and across the tides of criticism and biography that have since flooded around his name it is not easy to distinguish the poet from the almost legendary figure of Scottish history. Even people who have passed their lives in England south of the Tyne cannot conceive what Burns means to the majority of his fellow-countrymen: for he belongs to their national history in a sense in which Keats, say, or Wordsworth, or Shelley, has never seemed to belong to the history of England. Even in the twentieth century Scotland takes her Burns very seriously indeed, more seriously perhaps than she took him in the eighteenth century. The poet who preached "the glorious privilege of being independent" can still furnish apt tags for the use of Parliamentary members from the Clyde. His songs are still sung at work and play in the unchanged glens of his country by men, women, and chil-

43

dren whose race is very little altered since Burns hobnobbed with their forefathers: and he is the only poet in English literature whose anniversary is deliberately celebrated with feasting, drink, and song by thousands who hold his name and work in affectionate reverence.

Nevertheless, it was a shrewd observer who first remarked (with more than a spice of malice) that your true Scot will always prefer a bad poem by a Scotsman to a good poem by an Englishman. In the face of such a possibility it seems important that we should avoid attaching to the poet such penalties of greatness as may be peculiar to Scotland. Burns himself (who once stated that Ramsay's "Gentle Shepherd" was the most glorious poem ever written) argues very amiably in this connection:

. . . if a' the land
Would take the Muse's servants by the hand,
Not only hear, but patronise, befriend them
And where ye justly can commend, commend them;
And aiblins when they winna stand the test
Wink hard and say the folks hae done their best!

44

Would all the land do this, then I'll be caution
You'll soon hae poets of the Scottish nation.

Scotland has done a good deal of hard winking
since then. Burns has even had some of it
directed at himself, for ever since another great
Scot, Carlyle, with pardonable exaggeration,
described him as the most gifted soul of the
eighteenth century, the poet's champions, chiefly
his fellow-countrymen, have continued to ap-
plaud him something louder than the universal
roof of literature will consent to echo. And
in view of this exceptionally strong national
prejudice in his favor, as inevitably happens
when a man of genius is consistently overpraised
or mispraised by a band of noisy enthusiasts,
the rest of the world (or, in this instance, England, at least) has responded by thinking less
of Burns than he deserves. Like Byron and
Shelley, he has received a great deal of mere
lip-service for many reasons only secondarily
connected with his poetry. Too many people
(not all of them Scots) have approached his
book by way of his biography. These, as was

45

inevitable, have intensified particular aspects of his genius at the expense of others no less important, viewing him, for instance, as a social prodigy rather than as a literary phenomenon, as a simple, artless soul rather than as an exceptionally intelligent poet, an artist in words. Others again, seeking, in the cant phrase, "to throw further light on his work," have set that work on one side to pry with their musty candles among the darker corners of his life.

Thus, to an exceptional extent, even for one of the inheritors of unfulfilled renown, the criticism of Burns' work has been diluted with the gossip of a century (mostly irrelevant) concerning his amours and drinking-bouts. Now nothing so twists our opinion of a poet's work as a too strict regard for his biography, if only because it fails to make sufficient allowance for his inventive imagination. Our appreciation of, say, a love poem does not depend upon a biographical occasion from which it may possibly have sprung. Even when we know, as sometimes we do know, that a particular incident in the poet's life caused the writing of some

46

particular poem, it is still misleading in literary criticism (though not necessarily in biographical speculation) to relate the details of the event with those of the poem. This tendency of modern "psychological" criticism has done much to divert attention from Burns' poetry, *qua* poetry, towards his life; and we associate the fictions of an author's work with the actual facts of his life at the peril of misunderstanding both. At this period of time the facts of Burns' life are sufficiently familiar not to need repetition. He was a rake and a drunkard as well as a poet: his chief offenses as a man were partly mitigated by the fact that he appears to have suffered much from a troublesome conscience, for he had a great and lasting will toward good in spite of his greater weakness for evil, as these things accorded with the prevailing moral standards of his own age. Coleridge, with his usual searching insight, made all plain when he said that "Burns preached from the text of his own errors." Burns preached from other, larger but less interesting, texts as well—liberty, social justice, independence—but this was always his

47

most convincing sermon. And criticism of the biographical kind has laid too much stress on the text and the errors, and not enough on the literary qualities, of the sermon.

To the eyes of his contemporaries Burns was something more than a poet: he was a prodigy, picturesque and curious enough to excite interest in every grade of society. He was also a trumpet singing to that battle which every individual Scot wages against the rest of the world, the battle for personal independence. What John Barbour, in the thirteen-hundreds, had called Freedom, Burns called Independence. Barbour, as Sir Walter Raleigh has pointed out, was referring merely to freedom from imprisonment; Burns, of course, meant primarily spiritual and economic freedom, in his day as difficult to ensure as physical liberty was in the fourteenth century. Thus Barbour and Burns refer to equivalent evils.

> Ah! Fredome is a noble thing!
> Fredome mayse man to haif liking;
> Fredome all solace to man giffis,
> He livis at ese that frely livis!

48

A noble hart may haif nane ese,
Na elleys nocht that may him plese,
Gif fredome fail'th; for fre liking
Is yharnit ouer all othir thing.

Burns knew something of "the anger and the wretched doom that is couplit to foul thraldome." But four centuries wrought changes in the tune: the thraldom is of a different kind but no less objectionable for that.

If I'm designed yon lordling's slave,
By Nature's law designed,
Why was an independent wish
E'er planted in my mind?

Seen in the light of social history this is right enough. But—and it is best expressed colloquially—Burns appears to have lived in continual fear of "being put upon," and he guarded his independence with a fierce and jealous suspicion which finds constant expression in his work. At its best (though rather a too rhetorical and didactic best) this gospel of independence appears in his famous song "A man's a man for a' that."

49

Ye see yon birkie ca'd a lord
Wha struts, an' stares, an' a' that:
Tho' hundreds worship at his word
He's but a coof for a' that.
For a' that, an' a' that,
His ribband, star an' a' that,
The man o' independent mind
He looks an' laughs at a' that.

The creed of his gospel is expressed in one of
his English poems:

To catch Dame Fortune's golden smile,
    Assiduous wait upon her;
And gather gear by every wile
    That's justified by honour:
Not for to hide it in a hedge,
    Nor for a train attendant;
But for the glorious privilege
    Of being independent.

Such passages, though they may mark a period
in social history, are not of prime importance
in the history of poetry. Didactic verse never
showed Burns at his best, but the least successful of his didactic verse is that in which he tries
to write explicitly of his convictions regarding

50

independence and the social rights of man. Whenever his gospel ceases to be explicit it tends actually to spiritualize and dignify his poetry, for the contemporaneous feelings for "Liberty, Equality and Fraternity" were an inherent part of his attitude towards life and not the least ennobling quality of his work. But when Burns was bitter he was generally ineffectual. In the face of social injustice, snobbery or humbug he learned to temper his indignation with humour; and even such a little, off-side, good-humoured poem as the ode "To a Louse" (seen crawling on a Lady's bonnet in Church), with its famous moral, is more effective than most of his high-serious jibes at social inequalities.

> Ye ugly, creepin' blastit wonner,
> Detested, shunned by saint and sinner,
> How dare ye set your fit upon her
>   So fine a Lady!
> Gae somewhere else and seek your dinner
>   On some poor body.

Similarly, his attitude towards the "birkies" called Lords is much better suggested by the

"Lines on dining with Lord Daer," whom he admired, than by any of the usual class-conscious sneers we meet in his poems. "Last night, I dinnered wi' a Lord!"

> I've been at drucken Writers' feasts,
> Nay, been bitch-fou' 'mang godly Priests—
>   Wi' reverence be it spoken!—
> I've even joined the honour'd jorum,
> When mighty Squireships of the quorum,
>   Their hydra drouth did sloken.
>
> But wi' a Lord! Stand out my shin!
> A Lord—a Peer—an Earl's son?
>   Up higher yet my bonnet!
> And sic' a Lord! Lang Scotch ell twa',
> Our peerage he looks o'er them a',
>   As I look o'er my sonnet.

* * * * *

> I sidling sheltered in a neuk,
> An' at his Lordship staw a leuk,
>   Like some portentous omen;
> Except good sense and social glee,

An' (what surprised me) modesty,
  I markèd nought uncommon.

I watch'd the symptoms o' the Great,
The gentle pride, the lordly state,
  The arrogant assuming;
The fient a pride, nae pride had he,
Nor sauce, nor state, that I could see
  Mair than an honest ploughman.

Then from his Lordship I shall learn,
Henceforth to meet with unconcern
  One rank as well's another;
Nae honest, worthy man need care
To meet with noble youthfu' Daer,
  For he but meets a brother.

So, by preaching the national gospel of independence (with special reference to himself), Burns endeared himself to one-half of the heart —the pugnacious half—of his fellow-countrymen. By setting beautiful words to every known air of the folk he captured the other, tenderer half of their hearts. He was, at once, from the national point of view, a first-class poet and a people's poet, not a very common combination, and thus, remembering his picturesque origins and the familiar background, the landscape of his verse, not all his prodigious popularity has been due to the quality of his poetry, nor has interest in him survived for purely literary reasons. Herein lies the weakness of so much Scottish criticism concerning Burns. His poetry has been indiscriminately accepted, the good with the bad, while national opinion, contemplating Scottish literature with Burns in the foreground, has tried to wring out of the sight more self-gratification than is, perhaps, justified.

But after making all allowances for these present considerations, stripped of all his appeal to particular national sentiment, Burns still remains the finest poet, on the whole, between Milton and Wordsworth. And, setting aside mere lip-service, it appears that his poetry has never been *really* popular south of the Border country. The old explanation—that the dialect is too troublesome for the Southerner or the

American to master—will not pass. The same may be said, with equal untruth, of Chaucer's English, while, in point of fact, there are more unfamiliar words and obscure phrases in any five or six of Shakespeare's plays than in all Burns' works. The truth is, probably, that the English reader, very naturally, chooses to begin with Burns' non-dialect poems, and these, taken all together, comprise his least successful, least characteristic, least revealing work, and they therefore leave a false impression of his genius.

By something more than right of dates Burns belongs to the eighteenth century. In spite of all his fine truancies he had put himself to school with his English predecessors, Pope and Thomson, and he thought highly, as most people did then, of Shenstone. And though in practice he could never reconcile their teaching with his own poetic instincts, yet their influence is continuously apparent in his work, cheek by jowl with that of the old balladry.

These "English" poems contain a hundred indications as to the practical difficulties of authorship which, as a comparatively unlettered man, he had to overcome before he could create a fit literary medium out of his mother-tongue. Burns built his poetic house out of the rock of Scotland, but more than one of its architectural features derive from Twickenham and St. James's. A genuine reverence for the eighteenth century conventions of English verse engaged in a constant struggle with his instinctive tastes, which, of course, won in the end. Actually the quality of his non-dialect poems was not inferior to the general level of current English verse: but it was certainly inferior to his own average level. Burns, in spite of his characteristic pride and independence, was not without his share of that modesty which is so often secreted in self-educated men whose intelligence is in advance of their learning. He was very conscious of his defects, but, in some respects, unfortunately, he misunderstood his own genius. In all that concerned literature he had a very large respect for authority, reputation and tradition. Although he more than once attacked the schools—

A set o' dull conceited hashes
Confuse their brains in college classes!
They gang in stirks and come out asses,
   Plain truth to speak;
An' syne they think to climb Parnassus
   By dint o' Greek.

Gie me ae spark o' nature's fire,
That's a' the learning I desire;
Then—tho' I drudge thro' dub an' mire
   At pleugh or cart,
My muse, tho' homely in attire,
   May touch the heart.

although too, he saw himself in essential
moments as a poet whose work thrived best
when he approached it in his own language and
against his own national background, he was by
no means satisfied, in theory at least, with this
"ae spark o' nature's fire." Like many another
fine poet he did not doubt that the climb over
Parnassus would have been less formidable had
he carried some Greek with him. Thus, when
Coila, his native muse, addresses him in "The

Vision," he makes her praise certain English poets at his own and her expense:

> Thou canst not learn, nor can I show,
> To paint with Thompson's landscape glow,
> Or wake the bosom-melting throe
>   With Shenstone's art,
> Or pour with Gray the moving flow
>   Warm on the heart.

This is very bad Burns: but that "nor can I show," was no mere affectation of humility. Burns had only to remember one of these names, he had only to think, say, of Pope, and his mind, it seems, filled immediately with a hectoring consciousness of opportunities never presented and powers latent within him for lack of what he conceived to be the necessary food. Thus he could confess his regret at being "unacquainted with the necessary requisites for commencing poet by rule." His actual poetic practice leaves no cause to doubt the sincerity of his preface to the Kilmarnock Edition of his poems:

58

If any critic catches at the word genius, the author tells him, once for all, that he certainly looks upon himself as possest of some poetic abilities, otherwise his publishing in the manner he has done, would be a manœuvre below the worst character which, he hopes, his worst enemy will ever give him: but to the genius of a Ramsay or the glorious dawnings of the poor, unfortunate Fergusson, he, with equal unaffected sincerity, declares that, even in his highest pulse of vanity he has not the most distant pretensions.

Even after his Edinburgh successes, when all Scotland began to acclaim him, Burns gained very little in self-confidence, and, left to himself, lost nothing of this kind of humility. Luckily he had Ramsay and Fergusson and the old ballads to counterbalance his regard for Pope and Shenstone and the English generation of the time. Thus he was never dragged from the outer swirls into the central maelstrom of "eighteenth-century verse." Yet, whether or not art can be distinguished from feeling in

poetry, Burns had more of both than most of
the poets he honoured above himself. When
he fell out of English into his own language,
he invented rules of his own and rigorously applied them. Elsewhere, in commencing poet
by rule, he woke no throes and melted no
bosoms, but usually wrote flat verse of the kind
that might have qualified for a place in the
lower tiers of Dodsley's Miscellany:

> Why ye tenants of the lake
> For me your watery haunts forsake?
> Tell me, fellow-creatures, why
> At my presence thus you fly?
>
> Why disturb your social joys,
> Parent, filial, kindred ties?
> Common friend to you and me
> Nature's gifts to all are free.

And yet, though this may be the voice of Jacob,
the hands are not unlike those of Esau. It is,
however, a far cry from this kind of thing to
the spontaneous wistfulness of the famous poem

to a Mouse, though the theme is substantially the same as before:

> I'm truly sorry man's dominion
> Has broken nature's social union,
> And justifies that ill opinion
>   Which mak's thee startle
> At me, thy poor earth-born companion
>   And fellow-mortal.

English verse, as he knew it best, with its mannered subjections, froze his impulse, excepting when (as in this instance) he dropped momentarily out of dialect at a point where his own language merged into ours. So too, in the "Bard's Epitaph," he lapses, as it were unconsciously, into ordinary English without any noticeable change in the poetic quality.

> The poor inhabitant below
> Was quick to learn and wise to know,
> And keenly felt the friendly glow
>   And softer flame;
> But thoughtless follies laid him low
>   And stained his name.

But although, as we have seen, Burns was so

unself-confident as to be often intimidated by
the contemporary English rules, and even to
adopt them in his more self-conscious moods,
it was the manner, more than the matter, of his
work which was affected. Coila, though there
were things she could not show him, was, after
all, Burns' own muse, and he was never for
long unfaithful to her. His alien trafficking
may not have done much to improve his instinctive impulse towards poetry, but it was
valuable as discipline. His dialect poems might
have lacked much of their ease and economy
had he never attempted to write in the language
and manner of Pope and Shenstone. He
learned to catch more than the usual amount of
the Twickenham voice—

When Nature her great masterpiece designed
And framed her last, best work, the human mind,
Her eye intent on all the mazy plan,
She formed of various parts the various man.

But Burns never lost any of his essential poetic
individuality by such imitations. It is only

when he attempts complimentary *vers de société* that he ceases altogether to be himself.

One irritating and far-reaching effect of these English leanings was the attitude Burns learned to take up toward his own authorship. Here is a typical passage from his scrap book.

> . . . though the weather has brightened up a little with me, yet there has always been since a tempest brewing round me in the grim sky of futurity, which I pretty plainly see will some time or other, perhaps, ere long, overwhelm me, and drive me into some doleful dell, to pine in solitary, squalid wretchedness. . . . However, as I hope my poor country muse, who, all rustic, awkward and unpolished as she is, has more charms for me than any other pleasure of life beside—as I hope she will not then desert me, I may even then learn to be, if not happy, at least easy, and *south a song* to sooth my misery.

He was much too ready to describe himself as a rustic bard, a simple poet, an untutored rustic, "the hero of those artless strains," the

composer of uncouth rhymes. This habit has
drawn a most unfortunate trail across his subsequent reputation, for, by force of repetition,
this kind of false and sentimental description
has clung to his name ever since. Now it is true
that Burns was once a ploughman and he may
even have been a simple ploughman, though
those who have read between the lines of his
life will reserve judgment on this point. But
he was never a simple or an artless poet. Neither in his life, nor in his work, and least of all
in the salons of Edinburgh where he associated
on fairly equal terms with the flower of the
nation's intellect, in nothing scarcely, saving this
kind of self-description, does Burns appear artless or simple. For artless we should read "unaffected," for simple, "straightforward." He
never said or wrote or did anything that can
fairly be called humbug. No poet of his country, and very few in British literature, less
deserves such a description. The mistake comes
largely from the way in which superficial criticism has associated his name with those of such
"peasant-poets" as Bloomfield, Clare, Hogg and

Stephen Duck. With them Burns had nothing in common saving his origins. Their simplicity was of the mind as well as of the heart. It is best described as "simpleness." Their artlessness was an infantile quality deriving from the simpleness of their outlook upon life. They were not concerned with real values. They thought and wrote intuitively rather than consciously: their emotions and observation carried them through their poetry with only a minimum of art. But Burns, as Byron said "belongs to the very first rank of his art." He wrote like Wordsworth and Keats, governing a great instinctive impulse with imaginative conscious intelligence. To Clare or Bloomfield the shepherd on the horizon was a shepherd on the horizon, and he was nothing more: but Burns may fairly be said to have seen him, with more Wordsworthian eyes, as lonely Man plodding onwards against the background of the universe, a symbol of human power and spiritual immortality. His poetry, unlike theirs, touches sometimes upon the "thoughts that do often lie too deep for tears," and he had heard, though not so distinctly as Wordsworth, something of the "still, sad music of humanity."

> The best laid schemes of mice and men
>   Gang aft agley,
> And lea's us nought but grief and pain
>   For promised joy.
>
> Still thou art blest, compared wi' me!
> The present only toucheth thee:
> But och! I backward cast my e'e
>   On prospects drear!
> And forward, though I cannot see,
>   I guess and fear.

This is not the simplicity of a simple man. It is the simplicity of self-realization with all its usual universal significance. It is expressed with all the power of poetry emerging from feeling meditation upon the doubts and despairs of life. Keats, in his "Ode to a Nightingale," sees his world from something of the same angle:

> . . . what thou hast never known,
> The weariness, the fever and the fret
> Here, where men sit and hear each other groan;
> Where palsy shakes a few, sad, last, grey hairs,

66

Where youth grows pale and spectre-thin and
    dies. . . .

And Shelley has the same thought in his "Ode
to a Skylark":

> We look before and after,
>   And pine for what is not . . .

He made one of the finest similes for remembered grief in all our poetry:

> Still o'er these scenes my mem'ry wakes
>   And fondly broods with miser-care;
> Time but the impression stronger makes,
>   As streams their channels deeper wear.

He was sharp and shrewd and wise, with a very
real perception of human values which made
him the enemy of humbug and injustice in every
shape or form. There is neither artlessness nor
simplicity in his satirical verses. "Holy Willie's
Prayer" is a first-class example of satirical cunning as it is also of masterly versification and
deadly humour. Pope never wrote anything
more effective:

67

O Thou, that in the heavens does dwell,
Wha, as it pleases best Thysel',
Sends ane to heaven an' ten to hell,
  A' for Thy glory,
And no for ony guid or ill
  They've done afore Thee!

I bless and praise Thy matchless might,
When thousands Thou hast left in night,
That I am here afore Thy sight,
  For gifts an' grace
A burnin' and a shinin' light
  To a' this place.

O Lord, Thou kens what zeal I bear
When drinkers drink and swearers swear,
An' singing here an' dancin' there,
  Wi' great and sma';
For I am keepit by Thy fear
  Free frae them a'.

      *   *   *   *   *

Lord, mind Gaw'n Hamilton's deserts;
He drinks and swears and plays at cartes,
Yet has sae mony takin' arts,
  Wi' great and sma,

Frae God's own priests the people's hearts
He steals awa'.

An' when we chasten'd him therefor,
Thou kens how he bred sic a splore,
And set the warld in a roar
    O' laughing at us;—
Curse Thou his basket and his store,
Kail an' potatoes.

* * * * *

But, Lord, remember me an' mine
Wi' mercies temporal and divine,
That I for grace an' gear may shine,
    Excelled by nane,
And a' the glory shall be thine,
    Amen, Amen!

This is the simplicity of an artist in verse, not
of a "simple rustic." And even in Burns' songs,
where there is but little particularization to
coarsen the poetic texture, experience plays an
intellectual as well as an emotional part. For
mere emotion, however intense, does not write
poetry unaided by art: otherwise every growing
boy and girl would be writing good poetry, and

more than one of the simple ploughmen who
have broken the Scottish glebe since Burns' day
would be poets as good as he, while every English village would lose its mute, inglorious
Milton. In an age when every intelligent
undergraduate attempts verse and the word
"poet" is all too loosely used, it cannot be
merely platitudinous to recall that poetry is one
of the arts,—that it requires, in fact, a power of
expression in the maker as well as a capacity
for feeling. Burns was neither simple nor artless, and what may have been in him modesty,
or a shade too much of literary subservience to
great names, or humility in the face of his
knowledge of his own ignorance, or even of
self-compassion, declines into mere sentimental
stupidity on the part of those disciples and critics
and old ladies who have been content to take
the poet at his own underestimation. Burns'
intellect, as it appears in the foregoing quotations, was every whit as potent an instrument as
that of any poet who had won green laurels
since the days of Milton and Dryden. The
intellect of the great Pope himself, for all its
wider, because more educated, range, was, in

quality, no more keen or compelling or expansive than that of Burns, who, moreover, possessed in imaginative power and emotional sensitiveness a thousand heights and depths such as Pope never visited. Education, in the academic sense, Burns, of course, lacked, and therefore, according to eighteenth-century standards, something of that perception Addison called "taste." But Burns was a pioneer of a new taste that could mourn over the uprooting of a daisy, something almost symbolic of man's life ("He cometh up and is cut down like a flower"), or the shooting of a hare.

The art of poetry, as Burns found it in the latter half of the eighteenth century, was confined to a few variations of a dozen possible tunes on a one-stringed instrument. After more than a century of deliberate, thin monotone Burns brought music and poetry together again. And with the music of the old Scottish songs a thousand of the old themes of poetry returned to literature. We lost the voices of Phillis and Corydon and regained those of Helen of Kirconnell's lover and the Percy. Love and heartbreak return again to poetry.

Had we never loved sae kindly,
Had we never loved sae blindly,
Never met—nor ever parted,
We had ne'er been broken-hearted.

So too returns variety, and with a vengeance.
For Burns' variety is the greatest in eighteenth-
century poetry, and one of the most remarkable
in British literature. He wrote songs admittedly
second only to Shakespeare's, and each in its own
verse-form according to what the tune imposed
—and this was to secure and safeguard the folk-
poetry and folk-music of a nation. He matched
Chaucer on Chaucer's own peculiar ground with
the best narrative poem of its kind in our language, a poem so excellent that when Hazlitt,
in his lectures on the English poets, came to
Burns he disdained criticism and read "Tam o'
Shanter" from beginning to end. He wrote
satirical pieces which have stood the test of a
hundred years, within which the satires of Pope,
and even of Dryden, have lost much of their
ancient popularity, excepting, possibly, in the
eyes of those who set examination papers on
such subjects. He gave a fresh impulse to
Scottish patriotism, and presented the national

72

love of independence with a local habitation and a name. He wrote moral and didactic pieces which, in their own little realm of poetry, may be ranked fairly high. He set to music the short and simple annals of the poor and, in "The Cotter's Saturday Night," painted an enduring picture of that peasantry of earth who will never pass away. He translated the spirit of a nation into poetry. As an epistolary poet he has no peer. Humour, sense, good feeling, observation, good-fellowship, tumble all together in his epistles which are scattered with fine lyrical passages. In startling contrast to some of these achievements he wrote more than one ranting, joyous, amoral piece, of which "The Jolly Beggars" is the type, to the tune of

> A fig for those by laws protected,
>> Liberty's a glorious feast:
>> Courts for cowards were erected,
>> Churches built to please the priest.

And he wrote all these various kinds of poetry, at one time or another, surpassingly well, while remaining essentially a great lyric poet, thus making the best of all sides of Parnassus with

73

more than a spark of that divine carelessness and plenitude which appears so seldom in English literature outside the pages of Shakespeare himself. He maintained his poetic freshness and innocence to the end. Whatever calamities may have helped to stale his life, the dew always lay fresh upon his verse. Only in one respect, perhaps, can Burns be said to have failed. The chronological study of his work suggests that he never discovered what he was actually trying to discover, a medium of sufficient scope to employ his various capabilities to the full, all combining to serve a single purpose. He could acquit himself magnificently on any one of a score of different instruments, but he never attempted to rule the full orchestra. More than one poet with less skill than his has yet achieved more ambitious designs. If Burns had gone to London instead of to Edinburgh, where literary society and artistic practice gave him very little that he could not win for himself at home, he might have left an even greater mark on the history of poetry. As it is, only a "conscious" poet, the master of his art, could have achieved so much.

74

SOME MODERN POETS

THE POET LAUREATE

The Poet Laureate

ROBERT BRIDGES succeeded Alfred Austin as Poet Laureate of England in 1913. He was then in his seventieth year, having been born in 1844, four years after Thomas Hardy, and six years before Robert Louis Stevenson. Only two years ago, when he was eighty-one, he published a book of new poems breathing such warmth and power that it is hard to think of him as an octogenarian who won his first laurels only a little later than Meredith, Rossetti, and Swinburne. Mr. Bridges' first book was published in 1873 and followed at not very frequent intervals during the next two decades by various small volumes of sonnets and lyrics, and (excluding his dramas) at least one sustained piece, the narrative *Eros and Psyche*, a poem which has not been surpassed in its kind since Keats wrote *Lamia*. By 1898 these works had been collected with some other pieces to form his *Poetical Works*. But this edition was superseded in 1912 by an even larger collection when Mr. Bridges took his

79

place in the "Oxford Poets" series (most of whom, by the way, are really Cambridge poets edited at Oxford) published by the Clarendon Press. This volume remains the standard edition of his work, although it is not complete. It comprises the poet's two "Masks in the Greek Manner," *Eros and Psyche*, the not very sequential sequence of sonnets called *The Growth of Love*, some experimental pieces in quantitative verse, and the shorter lyrics that contain his finest work. Then, in 1919, after a virtual silence of fifteen years, his first laureate volume appeared—"*October and Other Poems.*" It included a group of "official" verses (war poems and others) which would not have discredited even the greatest of his predecessors in a not very enviable office. Thus the quantity of his work is not large for an authorship of more than fifty years. The rate of his production has been as leisurely as the mood of the production itself. What matters is the quality; and this Mr. Bridges has nursed with fewer lapses from virtual perfection than any living poet, excepting perhaps Mr. A. E.

Housman, who, quantitatively speaking, is the most meagre poet in English history.

Half a century, of course, has been time enough to break the crust of indifference and neglect which inevitably forms at first over poetry so unobtrusive as that of Mr. Bridges. Today the quality of his audience could scarcely be bettered, for it is known to include nearly all his distinguished English contemporaries, especially the poets, both old and young. But his achievement has yet to be realized by the ordinary reader of poetry in England, not to mention America, where, so far, his work is not well known outside the pages of the anthologies. (This is perhaps because the revival of American interest in poetry began after Mr. Bridges had written the greater part of his work, though that is not the best of reasons.) It may be that the English critics are to blame. Mr. Bridges has never been one of those hardy-annual poets whose new titles occur in the publishers' advertisements like fixed feasts in the Church calendar. Thus, more than most poets of today, he has needed critical advertisement by way of

introduction to the public at large. During the
past fifteen years, however, the critics have allowed his name to rest on its past laurels. With
the exception of a small book by the English
poet and novelist, Mr. Francis Brett Young,
and a long, tender appreciation by Mr. J. C.
Squire, I know of very little that has been written concerning Mr. Bridges' work except in the
way of mere lip-service. Other critics have
tended to ignore his achievement in print even
when they admired it in private. (An exception must be made, however, in favor of Mr.
Llewellyn Jones, the Chicago critic, who has
split several lances on his behalf.)

This essay will perhaps prove to be a practical illustration of the reasons for the critical
silence. It is not easy to write about poetry like
that of Mr. Bridges without making both it and
your comments look a little insubstantial. In
the presence of pure poetry, criticism dwindles
(or expands, according to the way you look at
it) into plain appreciation. Thus there has been
little or no criticism of sheer song. You cannot
argue about a tune; you like it or you don't.

THE POET LAUREATE

In a harbour grene asleep whereas I lay
The byrdes sang swete in the middes of the day,
I dreamed fast of mirth and play:
In youth is pleasure, in youth is pleasure.

Wever's song is the type from which Mr.
Bridges' poetry mostly springs.

She too that loveth awaketh and hopes for thee;
Her eyes already have sped the shades that flee,
Already they watch the path thy feet shall take:
Awake, O heart, to be loved, awake, awake!

But critics, in general, prefer to argue; hence,
they have had very little to say about Mr.
Bridges, and many people who habitually read
poetry have not been led to his work. It cannot now be long before they find their own way.

It also seems likely that many are a little
suspicious of a poet who bears the laureate's
title. Even those who have never personally
acquainted themselves with the

Birthday torrents from Parnassus
And New Year's spring-tide of molasses

written by laureates like Pye and Tate, are

83

traditionally suspicious of an "official poet." A
glance at Mr. Bridges' book should be enough
to set them right. Not more than a score of
pseudo-official pieces appear in the two small
volumes which he has published during the
fifteen years of his laureateship; even these are
voluntary, not enforced tasks, and the poet, not
the laureate, is in the ascendant for the most
part. Witness the poetic quality of the sonnet
he wrote for the opening of the theatre of the
Royal Academy of Dramatic Art in London.

England will keep her dearest jewel bright,
And see her sons like to their sires renown'd:
Whose Shakespeare is with deathless Homer
        crown'd,
Her freedom the world's hope thron'd in the height.
All gifts of spirit are of such airy flight
That if their fire be spent they fall to ground:
Their virtue must with newborn life abound
And by young birth renew their old birthright.

We workers therefore in this troublous age
Would keep our beauty of language from misfeature,
Presenting manners noble and mirth unblamed:

84

So Truth shall walk majestic on our stage,
And, when we hold the mirror up to Nature,
She, seeing her face therein, shall not be ashamed.

Not many laureates have achieved so much in parallel circumstances.

And, lastly, because of the poet's secondary interest in the old controversy concerning the problems of an Anglo-Classic prosody, as well as his curious experiments in quantitative and accentual verse, others believe him to be an eccentric litterateur, one who is interested less in the spirit than in the mechanics of poetry. There is scarcely a shred of real justification for such a mistake. Mr. Bridges himself has always taken pains to distinguish the experimental part of his work from the rest. But even his confessed exercises are those of a poet, not of a mere prosodist. Parts of his line-for-line paraphrase of a famous passage from the Aeneid, for instance, are not only fine translation: they also exist as poetry in their own right.

There miserably fellow'd in death's indignity saw he
Leucaspis with his old Lycian seachieften Orontes,

Whom together from Troy in homecoming over the
    waters
Wild weather o'ermastered, engulfing both shipping
    & men.
And lo! his helmsman, Palinurus, in eager emotion,
Who on the Afric course, in bright starlight, with a
    fair wind
Fell by slumber opprest unheedfully into the wide
    sea.

No mere prosodist could have risen to the
climax of the concluding line. Even here, however, the poet is not so well at ease as when he
is singing his own song, even though it be in
Neo-Miltonic Syllabics (his latest invention,
still peculiar to himself, which, he says in the
preface to *New Verse*, "pretends to offer their
true desideratum to the advocates of Free
Verse"), or in the accentual sonnet to Francis
Jammes, in which there is nothing to show where
the prosodist ends and the poet begins—

You are here in spirit, dear poet, and bring a motley
    group,
Your friends afore you sat stitching your heavenly
    trousseau—

86

The courteous old road mender, the queer Jean
    Jacques Rousseau,
Columbus, Confucius, all to my English garden they
    troop,
Under his goatskin umbrella the provident Robinson
    Crusoe,
And the ancestor dead long ago in Domingo or
    Guadaloupe.

Even this is merely Mr. Bridges riding his
private hobby-horse with the skill of one who
has elsewhere ridden a winged steed. Much of
this experimental work, of course, will appeal
chiefly to the student of prosody. But it bulks
very little in Mr. Bridges' canon and need not
detain us here except while we insist that the
ordinary reader must look to the shorter lyrical
poems to find this poet's feeling moving in complete accord with his skill.

The impulses that conspire to make a poet,
especially a lyric poet, seem most often to
originate in some kind of spiritual dissatis-
faction. Whatever moods may result in his
writing, psychological criticism can usually trace

them to this source. "We think caged birds sing when indeed they cry," says Flamineo in Webster's tragedy: and the thought fits most of the great lyric poets from Sappho to the author of "A Shropshire Lad." In our own time, at least, very few English poets have inclined to look at life without a wry face. There are a few possible exceptions, like Mr. Ralph Hodgson, though even his half dozen great poems have an undercurrent of sadness. Both Mr. James Stephens and Mr. W. H. Davies sing with a certain Celtic gaiety in places: but the joy of one is more faery than human, while the other in his happiness too frequently recalls the famous cow in the corn. Mr. Bridges is the exception *par excellence*. The peculiar originality of his work is its dominating mood of eager delight, a mood that sparkles with implications of genuine spiritual fulfilment, the outcome of a faith repeatedly expressed, that

> in spite of woe and death,
> Gay is life and sweet is breath.

The basis of his mood is contentment . . .

88

   . . . every eve I say,
Noting my step in bliss,
That I have known no day
In all my life like this.

Even his love poetry is the poetry of fulfilled
love.

Since thou, O fondest and truest,
Hast loved me best and longest,
And now with trust the strongest
The joy of my heart renewest ...

One rejoicing lyric after another etches the
character of a happy life, until, in his old age,
the poet epitomizes his philosophy in the quiet
valedictory lyric "Fortunatus Nimium"—

I have lain in the sun,
I have toiled as I might,
I have thought as I would
And now it is night.

My bed full of sleep,
My heart of content
For mirth that I met
The way that I went.

89

I welcome fatigue
While frenzy and care
Like thin summer clouds
Go melting in air.

To dream as I may
And awake when I will,
With the songs of the birds
And the sun on the hill.

Or death—were it death,
To what should I wake,
Who loved in my home
All life for its sake?

What good have I wrought?
I laugh to have learned
That joy cannot come
Unless it be earned:

For a happier lot
Than God giveth me,
It never hath been,
Nor ever shall be.

The greater part of his lyric poetry, like this, is

the exquisitely simple expression of a positive
joy: that is, it stands in complete opposition to
that negative "poetry of escape" of which Mr.
de la Mare's lovely work (especially its later
phases) is the best modern example.

A series of lyric affirmations, compounding
reason, worship, and joy in serene and urbane
verse, is strangely alien to the spirit of our age,
though not to what Mr. Bridges himself has
called (in the title of his precious anthology)
the spirit of man. Very few English poets, living or dead, have caught such accents of sheer
delight as make the pulsating music of

Awake, the land is scattered with light, and see,
Uncanopied sleep is flying from field and tree:
And blossoming boughs of April in laughter shake;
Awake, O heart, to be loved, awake, awake!

or

> Love on my heart from heaven fell,
> Soft as the dew on flowers of spring,
> Sweet as the hidden drops that swell
> Their honey-throated chalicing.

or, "To the Nightingales,"

Beautiful must be the mountains whence ye come,
And bright in the fruitful valleys the streams, where-
  from ye learn your song:
Where are those starry woods? O might I wander
  there
Among the flowers, which in that heavenly air
  Bloom the year long!

(Though in this last extract there is an accent
of longing which does not often occur in his
work.) His finest sonnet touches the edge of
rapture.

I would be a bird, and straight on wings I arise,
And carry purpose up to the ends of the air:
In calm and storm my sails I feather, and where
By freezing cliffs the unransomed wreckage lies:
Or, strutting on hot meridian banks surprise
The silence: over plains in the moonlight bare
I chase my shadow, and perch where no bird dare
In treetops torn by the fiercest winds of the skies.
Poor simple birds, foolish birds, then I cry,
Ye pretty pictures of delight, unstir'd
By the only joy of knowing that ye fly;
Ye are not what ye are, but rather, sum'd in a word

92

The alphabet of a god's idea, and I
Who master it, I am the only bird.

The mood is not always so explicit as this.
Delight is no less the current of feeling in such
"descriptive" poems as the one beginning

Flame-throated robin on the topmost bough
Of the leafy oak, what singest thou?

and in "A Passer-By."

Whither, O splendid ship, thy white sails crowding,
Leaning across the bosom of the urgent West,
That fearest not sea rising, nor sky clouding,
Whither away, fair rover, and what thy quest?

The very music implies it.

Thus Mr. Bridges has written poetry in one
of its very rarest moods, a "L'Allegro" cool
and refreshing after the continual "Il Penseroso" of most modern verse. He seldom
dwells for long on the darker realities. His
characteristic cry is "Think not that I can stain
my heaven with discontent" . . .

93

. . . while Reason lives
To mark me from the beast,
I'll teach her serve at least
To heal the wound she gives.

Even a poem called "Dejection," beginning with deep pessimism revolving thoughts of distress and death, he suddenly interrupts with

O soul, be patient, thou shalt find
A little matter mend all this;
Some strain of music to thy mind,
Some praise for skill not spent amiss.

Again shall pleasure overflow
Thy cup with sweetness; thou shalt taste
Nothing but sweetness, and shalt grow
Half sad for sweetness run to waste.

That "sweetness run to waste" is often the basis of his half-melancholy moods. Again in his "Elegy among the Tombs," he even attempts to reconcile joy with death itself. Could we see beyond death, he says, and so

With brightest visions our fond hopes repair;
Or crown our melancholy with despair;

94

From death, still death, still would a comfort come;
Since of this world the essential joy must fall
In all distributed, in each thing some,
In nothing all, and all complete in all;
Till pleasure, ageing to her full increase,
Puts on perfection and is throned in peace.

Thus he speculates that joy may be apotheosized
in death, only to break into the apostrophe

Thou art sweet peace, and thee I cannot fear.
Nay, were my last hope quenched, I here would sit
And praise the annihilation of the pit.

(The poem has a certain Shakespearean tone.)

But all this is not to suggest that Mr. Bridges
is merely one more easy optimist who supports
a comfortable philosophy by refusing to recognize uncomfortable facts. On the contrary,
some of his most impressive poems face the
darkest reality, the most catastrophic of all facts,
not with a useless, blustering challenge, for he
knows that

Only men incredulous of despair,
Half taught in anguish, through the midnight air

Beat upward to God's throne in loud access
Of shrieking and reproach . . .

but with the resigned serenity that ennobles
similar passages in poets as great as Milton,
Sophocles, and Shakespeare. Death, age, and
pain are the rarest words in Mr. Bridges'
vocabulary, and even rarer subjects of his verse.
Once or twice he refers to

The body, and the thing which perisheth;
The soil, the smutch, the toil, the ache and wear,
The grinding enginry of blood and breath,
Pain's random darts, the heartless spade of death.

His vocation as a physician must have given him
more than a mere library acquaintance with
these. Yet, when he definitely approaches the
horizons of existence in his poetry it is not to
abandon the courageous philosophy of "Fortunatus Nimium."

Daily thy life shortens, the grave's dark peace
  Draweth surely nigh,
  When goodnight is goodbye;
And the sleeping shall not cease.

96

Fight to be found fighting; nor far away
  Deem, nor strange thy doom.
  Like this sorrow 'twill come
And the day will be today.

This, I believe, is the only occasion when he permits himself to premeditate his own death. It sustains the mood of the dying man in "Winter Nightfall."

    He thinks of his morn of life,
      His hale, strong years;
    And braves as he may the night
      Of darkness and tears.

But in the poem "On a Dead Child" the imaginative realization of death is intensified to a point where the soliloquizing poet reaches the limits of his philosophy and all his tenderness for life gathers to help him utter his last word about Death as it had already done, perhaps with less finality of actual utterance, in the poem beginning "I never shall love the snow again."

So quiet! doth the change content thee?—Death,
    whither hath he taken thee?

To a world, do I think, that rights the disaster of
    this?
          The vision of which I miss
Who weep for the body, and wish but to warm thee
    and awaken thee?

Ah! little at best can all our hopes avail us
To lift this sorrow, or cheer us, when in the dark,
          Unwilling, alone we embark,
And the things we have seen and have known and
    have heard of, fail us.

Confronted by the perennial theme of mortality, the trial by fire which every poet, sooner
or later, must pass, Mr. Bridges excels himself.
We can compare his utterance with the greatest
and it lacks nothing. The joyful moods of a
poet who can realize disaster in these terms certainly do not spring from any complacent optimism. These elegies, and a few poems of
which "Pater Filio" is the finest, reveal the poet
in those rare moments when he betrays his
realization of the worm, the canker, and the
grief; he saddens over

Sense with keenest edge unused,
Yet unsteeled with scathing fire;
Lovely feet as yet unbruised
On the ways of dark desire;
Sweetest hope that lookest smiling
O'er the wilderness defiling!

Why such beauty to be blighted
By the swarm of foul destruction?
Why such innocence delighted,
When sin stalks to thy seduction?
All the litanies e'er chanted
Shall not keep thy faith undaunted.

But Mr. Bridges' faith, though sometimes daunted by such thoughts, is never shaken to its roots; and the result is a poetry that, while it can weep without whining, more often rejoices without beating a drum.

I have already suggested that the undercurrents of Mr. Bridges' happier mood can be traced through some of his descriptive lyrics. It is no less interesting to notice the similar undercurrents of his melancholy in certain others. At the outset, of course, we must re-

member that there is no such thing as a purely
"descriptive" poetry. Pictorial verse, like that
in which Mr. Bridges has reflected the English
landscape, rises into poetry by virtue of the
author's colouring mood or not at all. Minute
observation and skilful word painting, however
finely wrought, are not in themselves enough
to raise it. The absence of any direct emotional
statement must somehow be counterbalanced,
and this can only be done by means of implication, musical or metaphorical. It is not enough
merely to record appearances in the manner of
the poet who wrote

> Greatly shining,
> The Autumn moon floats in the thin sky;
> And the fish ponds shake their backs and flash their
>   dragon scales
> As she passes over them.

In this there is neither direct emotional statement nor yet implication. The words may be
chosen meticulously, and carefully brushed on
the canvas, but they have no reference. Was
the writer glad or sorry, moved by delight or

100

disgust? The reader can only speculate. Even an interested and observant fish, seeing the autumn moon from those same ponds, could scarcely look up with such cold-blooded neutrality. The same fault is frequently found in the work of English landscape poets when they paint the streaks of the tulip, like John Clare, and, in our own time, Mr. Edmund Blunden. But Mr. Bridges, even when he is most the painter, never falls into it. His descriptive verse is rife with implications. These are never "metaphorical" (like the implications made, for instance, by such poems as Mr. Robert Frost's "Mending Wall," or Mr. de la Mare's "The Moth," to name no more); they are always musical. For Mr. Bridges writes verse in as many different keys as Schubert used in song. You cannot doubt the delight of the observer who sings in such an obvious major as

Wanton with long delay the gay spring leaping
    cometh;
The blackthorn starreth now his bough on the eve
    of May;

All day in the sweet box-tree the bee for pleasure
     hummeth;
The cuckoo sends afloat his note in the air all day.

It leaps in the concealed rhymes, the alliteration, and the eager rhythm; but the poem contains no direct statement of this happy mood. It is all implied by a certain awareness in the tones of the verse. Nor, on the other hand, is the poet's darker mood less immediately apparent in the perfect stanzas on the felling of the oak.

> The hill pines were sighing,
> O'ercast and chill was the day:
> A mist in the valley lying
> Blotted the pleasant May.
>
> But deep in the glen's bosom
> Summer slept in the fire
> Of the odorous gorse blossom
> And the hot scent of the brier.
>
> A ribald cuckoo clamoured,
> And far in the copse the stroke

Of the iron axe that hammered
The iron heart of the oak.

Anon a sound appalling
As a hundred years of pride
Crashed, in the silence falling;
And the shadowy pine-trees sighed.

This is the minor key, of which we have already
heard a whisper in "Nightingales" and the full
diapason in the elegies. His descriptive verse
ranges variously between these two extremes,
and the mood of each poem is definitely recog-
nizable by its key no less than if it were one
of his lyrics of direct statement, like

One grief of thine
    if truth be confest
Was joy to me;
    for it drave to my breast
Thee, to my heart
    to find thy rest.

How long it was
    I never shall know;
I watcht the earth

So stately and slow,
And the ancient things
  that waste and grow.

But now for me
  what speed devours
Our heavenly life,
  our brilliant hours!
How fast they fly,
  the stars and flowers!

Such, then, are the outstanding characteristics of Mr. Bridges' poetry. Its easy and conventional appearance only superficially disguises what is actually a remarkable originality. There is nothing very novel, of course, in the poet's attitude, which has already been described by another critic as "the philosophy of the average man." The originality lies rather in the way that philosophy is reflected in his verse. Mr. Bridges has given us what every poet must try to give, something "common in experience, but uncommon in expression," to borrow the phrase in which Mr. Robert Frost improves on Pope's famous "What oft was thought but ne'er so well expressed." He has never looked far afield for the material of his poetry. It lay ready around him—the southern English landscape, the felling of a tree, the sailing of a ship, the return of spring, the delight of love, the death of a dear friend, the sight of a dead child, the bare joy of being alive on an "idle June day on the sunny Thames."

I would have life—thou saidst—all as this day,
Simple enjoyment, calm in its excess,
With not a grief to cloud and not a ray
Of passion overhot my peace to oppress;
With no ambition to reproach delay,
Nor rapture to disturb its happiness . . .

and a thousand memories of rare moments captured, like that lovely poem in *New Verse* where the aged poet remembers himself a schoolboy lying awake, listening to the rustle of rain in the trees on a summer night and the murmur of voices passing his window—so that even today

> Into the maze of my delight
> Those blind intruders walk;

105

And ever I wonder who they be
And of what things they talk.

All these things are so common in experience
that every poetaster has attempted some of
them. But they are transformed by a poet who,
in "When my love was away," actually matched
one of Wordsworth's best poems and struck the
great epic note in

I heard great Hector sounding war's alarms,
Where thro' the listless ghosts chiding he strode,
As tho' the Greeks besieged his last abode
And he his Troy's hope still, her king-at-arms.

Even the brief quotations that load this appreciation witness the variety and delicacy of a
verbal and metrical command which is one of
the richest in the whole range of English
literature, passing from the magically painted
subtleties of "London Snow" to the exquisite
simplicity of

Long are the hours the sun is above
But when evening comes I go home to my love . . .

a poem that continues through one surprising

variation after another of an exceptionally difficult metre. Mr. Bridges has certainly deserved his reputation as a "poets' poet." Surrounded as we are by so much that is slipshod in literature, we may count not least among his virtues the delight the Poet Laureate takes in his art. Even his consistent eccentricities have their value. His archaic verb and pronoun forms probably appear musty to people with fixed ideas concerning "poetic diction." More subtle ears will not fail to recognize the value of the old mode, because it not only subserves the delicacy of his verbal music, but also ministers to that urbane tone which is the most noticeable characteristic of his poetic style.

In this last word, style, we come to the culminating point of the Poet Laureate's achievement. There are many living poets whose work embraces a larger area of human experience than that of Mr. Bridges: many, too, are more ambitiously intellectual; and others, again, more apparently "up-to-date" than he— though, by the way, the author of these quiet

country pieces and love lyrics is one of the very
few living poets whose education and bread-
and-butter experience have leaned on the scientific side of knowledge, and it has yet to be
demonstrated that "up-to-date" poets go further than other kinds. (We need only to remember how Tennyson has been damned by
certain living critics for no better reason than
that he tried to be up-to-date so far as he knew
how.) But how many of these poets, like Mr.
Bridges, have style enough to betray their
authorship to the right reader, given an un-
signed manuscript? Mr. Hardy, Mr. Housman, Mr. Yeats, Mr. Frost, Mr. de la Mare
—are there any others? A few, like Mr.
Kipling and Mr. Masefield, might perhaps be
recognized by characteristic allusions, manner-
isms, peculiarities of argument or language, but
not, I think, by this, the most durable of all
identification marks in the arts. The type of
Mr. Bridges' poetry is not new in English—
whose is? Certain strains of his music have
been heard before, not only in Spenser and
Campion, but even in Milton himself. But

these and all the derivations of his work are merged by a style that cannot be mistaken for another's. It has some of the rarest attributes, clarity almost approaching perfection, great simplicity even when it is expressing very delicate shades of meaning, a continual glow from the core, and, everywhere, exceptional economy.

> It seem'd the hour had gather'd up
> For every sense a bliss
> To crown the faith of all desire
> With one assuaging kiss.

The resulting poetry, like this, is of the kind easiest to read but from a purely technical point of view hardest to write. It is a poetry that re-informs the old familiar themes with new feeling and original significance, that triumphs over the prosaic, trembling responsively to the mere chiaroscuro of human emotion as well as to its great flushes of color and light; a poetry that, whether delighted or dejected, is still quiet and self-sufficient, always beginning with a deep plunge into music and a straight, clean swim to the banks of silence. Mr.

Bridges utterly justifies the only lines resembling a boast that can be found in his work.

> Me whom thou sawest of late strive with the pains
> Of one who spends his strength to rule his nerve,
> —Even as a painter breathlessly who strains
> His scarcely moving hand lest it should swerve—
> Behold me, now that I have cast my chains,
> Master of the art which for thy sake I serve.

It is beyond dispute that the Poet Laureate is master of his art. We may look down the list of his great predecessors, to Tennyson, Wordsworth, Dryden, further back still to the times when Ben Jonson and even Spenser wore—perhaps not officially, but no less bravely for that—the laurels which have never been more fresh and green than they are today; but not even among these older and greater poets shall we find one who can more truthfully be called a master of his art than Robert Bridges.

WALTER DE LA MARE

Walter de la Mare

WHAT appears to be Mr. Walter de la Mare's final conversion from verse to imaginative prose as the medium of his most ambitious work is a portentous sign of the literary times. It is hard to believe that a poet of his genius, one moreover whose skill in the management of verse is nothing short of phenomenal, can be content to confine himself permanently to prose narrative. But it is some six years since Mr. de la Mare has published a volume of serious verse and his name no longer appears under isolated poems in the periodical press. During that time he has given us several volumes of exceptionally rich prose—short stories, at least one long romance, and several puzzling fragments, all woven no less subtly and poetically than the finest of his verse.

Yet, before that time—and, to some lovers of his work, even now—his importance as an author rested chiefly on his verse. He had always cherished an intermittent passion for writing prose romance. But in poetry he had achieved an unmistakable style of his own, and, like all good poets, had invented a world equally his own, a world whose atmosphere could not be matched for sheer magical color by any living poet. Then, with the publication of his "Memoirs of a Midget" he suddenly switched his poetry—style, world, atmosphere, and all—out of verse into prose.

Possibly in an age when only a few scattered readers are artistically educated up to the point where interest in a long poem can challenge the autocratic reign of the novel, a poet cannot safely rely on the faithfulness of an audience which, we are constantly told, will neither buy nor read long works in verse. Small blame if he attempts to adapt some more popular literary form to his poetic ends. Mr. de la Mare's prose amply demonstrates his faithfulness to the spirit of poetry. But verse has lost—one hopes only temporarily—one of its greatest living masters, and those who hold it to be a more interesting and fascinating form of literature have cause to lament the loss.

It is difficult to believe that verse is permanently ceasing to be the natural vehicle for extended works of the poetic imagination. Yet Thomas Hardy, in an earlier generation, drove his poetry to the market of prose fiction and bartered it there until he could afford his triumphant return to Parnassus. Like Mr. de la Mare he has always been a poet at heart. But it is interesting (if a little idle) to speculate what English poetic literature lost as a result. No doubt if Shakespeare himself had lived in this century he too would have adapted the novel to his purposes, as, in his own day, he adapted the readiest means. But poetry in prose can never be quite the same exciting and delightful thing as poetry in verse. Let the doubtful compare, say, Mr. de la Mare's curiously lovely fragment "The Connoisseur" with one or another of his finer poems—"The Old Angler," "The Last Coachload," "Farewell," or "Arabia."

This, of course, may not be the whole story concerning his change of garb. It can be justified from a purely technical point of view if we believe that the prose medium has enabled his genius to expand more freely than would have been possible in protracted verse of the kind he would have been likely to write. There has always been a certain quality of heaviness even in his shortest lyrics, and especially in his maturer verse; an excessively concentrated essence of poetry which might possibly be too rich and thick (like some almost solid liquid) to pour into the mould of a long poem. His tendency has always been to choke his form with substance. Every line of his later poems is packed to the point of bursting. Thus the very irregularities of prose, its side channels of parenthesis and circumlocution, may have offered a fuller liberty to a poet who realized his need of some less constricted form for such exceedingly constricted matter. But this is so much speculation and, true or false, irrelevant to the essential criticism of his work.

It is now twenty-seven years since Mr. de la Mare first took to print under the alluring pseudonym "Walter Ramal" which he later abandoned in favour of his real and even lovelier Huguenot name. His first book, *Songs*

of Childhood (1901), was succeeded by a
silence lasting five years. Then appeared *Poems*
and, after a further five years' silence, *The
Listeners* and *Peacock Pie*, which were published
almost simultaneously. Mr. de la Mare's verse
is perhaps best known by these two volumes and
Motley, a later war volume. *The Veil* (in my
opinion his finest book) completes the list, except for a recent small volume of nonsense
rhymes conceived in the mood of his earliest
work.

Most readers appear to regard Mr. de la
Mare primarily as a poet who writes for children. Others would enlarge his appeal to include (in the poet's own phrase, employed on
the title page of his astonishing anthology *Come
Hither*) "the young of all ages." But unless
that phrase can be interpreted to admit even
the most mellowed readers of poetry, people
concerned with the largest significances of life
in art, who look for deep meaning, values, high
imagination as well as skill and charm in the
verse they read—unless the man who loves
Wordsworth side by side with Campion, Chris-

tina Rossetti, and Robert Louis Stevenson can be included in this category, it must be dismissed.

Songs of Childhood, with the exception of one or two pieces like "Haunted" and "The Pilgrim" which quietly anticipate the more complex character of his later work, cannot be mistaken for anything but a collection of nursery rhymes and poems, ingenious and delicious verses like—

"Bunches of grapes," says Timothy;
"Pomegranates pink," says Elaine;
"A junket of cream and a cranberry tart
    For me," says Jane.

"Love-in-a-mist," says Timothy;
"Primroses pale," says Elaine;
"A nosegay of pinks and mignonette
    For me," says Jane.

"Chariots of gold," says Timothy;
"Silvery wings," says Elaine;
"A bumpity ride in a waggon of hay
    For me," says Jane.

and the lovely

> Down-adown-derry
>   Sweet Annie Maroon,
> Gathering daisies
>   In the meadows of Doone,
> Hears a shrill piping
>   Elf-like and free,
> Where the waters go brawling
>   In rills to the sea;
> Singing down-adown-derry.

But even so early as 1901 Mr. de la Mare had invented that glamorous, magical atmosphere which culminates in his volume *The Veil*. "Tartary" is not unlike a thin version of his famous "Arabia."

> Lord of the fruits of Tartary,
>   Her rivers silver pale!
> Lord of the hills of Tartary,
>   Glen, thicket, wood, and dale!
> Her flashing stars, her scented breeze,
> Her trembling lakes, like foamless seas,
> Her bird-delighting citron-trees
>   In every purple vale!

119

Here, however, there is nothing symbolic, no suggestion of a secondary significance as in the later poems. The book is crowded with miniatures of his more serious work, faint foreshadowings of the poet's full-grown imagination, as, for instance—

> How large unto the tiny fly
> Must little things appear!—
> A rosebud like a feather-bed,
> Its prickle like a spear.
>
> A dewdrop like a looking-glass,
> A hair like golden wire,
> The smallest grain of mustard-seed
> As fierce as coals of fire.
>
> A loaf of bread, a lofty hill,
> A wasp, a cruel leopard;
> And specks of salt as bright to see
> As lambkins to a shepherd.

This is actually an epitome of his great romance, *The Memoirs of a Midget*, written in prose some twenty years later. In 1901 Mr. de la Mare had already looked at the world through the eyes of his ultimate heroine, Miss M.

But in *Poems,* his second book, he leaves the nursery almost entirely only to return at odd moments through the rest of his poetic journey, and even then (as in some of the poems in *Peacock Pie*) seldom with quite the same innocent music on his lips. The fact that children delight in much of his later work is a flattering but nevertheless secondary consideration. Its underlying significance seems to escape them.

> . . . all the strident horror of
> Horse and rider in red defeat,
> Is only music fine enough
> To lull (them) into slumber sweet
> In fields where ewe and lambkin bleat.

Other writers of children's verse cease at the point where the essential Mr. de la Mare begins. Those who have coupled his name with the names of Mr. A. A. Milne and Robert Louis Stevenson completely mistake this poet.

This common misunderstanding is not only

due to the fact that the poems which first won Mr. de la Mare his current popularity were the admitted nursery rhymes and children's poems of his earliest books. Even his later work contains certain elements which are usually associated with fairy-tales and many of his most deeply significant poems have the superficial appearance of his earlier pieces. He has always been attracted by the more grotesque, fantastic, and curious appearances of people and things. The heroine of his chief prose work is a delicate fay-like creature, a midget, and its hero a misshapen dwarf. Similarly there is usually some faint strangeness about the people who inhabit his verse. They are like people remembered in a dream.

> When thin-strewn memory I look through,
> I see most clearly poor Miss Loo,
> Her tabby cat, her cage of birds,
> Her nose, her hair, her muffled words,
> And how she would open her green eyes,
> As if in some immense surprise. . . .

This is the mildest possible example. For the

full glamour of the dream-like quality in which
his poetry is saturated we must look less to the
particular figures it contains (many of them are
mere symbols for abstractions) than to the
atmosphere of the world they inhabit. It is
the atmosphere of a world hushed in mysterious, but slightly sinister calm, the world that
surrounds the silent house in "The Listeners,"
and like that house and the woods in "The Last
Coachload" thronged with invisible presences,
unheard whispers.

. . . marvellous peace and amity breathed there.
Tranquil the labyrinths of this sundown wood.
Musking its chaces, bloomed the brier-rose fair;
Spellbound as if in trance the pine trees stood.

Everything stands like those pine trees, "spellbound, as if in trance." When movement begins
all noises sound with a muted chime. No two
scenes in his verse are ever alike, yet brooding
behind all their appearances is the same invisible spirit, the same sense of melancholy calm.
There may be a hint as to its nature in
"Mirage."

123

Noonday to night the enigma of thine eyes
Frets with desire the travel-weary brain,
Till in the cast of dark the ice-cold moon arise
    And pour them peace again;
And with malign mirage uprears an isle
Of fountain and palm, and courts of jasmine and
    rose,
Whence far decoy of siren throats beguile,
    And maddening fragrance flows.
Lo, in the milken light, in tissue of gold
Thine apparition gathers in the air—
Nay, but the seas are deep, and the round world old,
    And thou art named, Despair.

Moreover, in this atmosphere there is frequently a vague sense of supernatural forces
lurking invisibly. To Mr. de la Mare the gulf
between reality and unreality is so small that he
can doubt whether our waking life is more real
than our dream life. The shapes and shadows
of both lives enter into the world of his poetry.
The reader, entering that world, ceases to tread
on anything resembling solid earth. He walks
with the princes in "Arabia" at noon under the
ghost of the moon. He is lost in some dream-

land halfway between the candid light and air
of day and the mysterious glow and shadow of
night, lost among whispering shades and heavy
colours.

> In the woods as I did walk,
> Dappled with the moon's clear beam,
> With a Stranger I did talk,
> And his name was Dream.
>
> Spurred his heel, dark his cloak,
> Shady-wide his bonnet's brim;
> His horse beneath a silvery oak
> Grazed as I talked with him.
>
> Softly his breast-brooch burned and shone;
> Hill and deep were in his eyes;
> One of his hands held mine, and one
> The fruit that makes men wise.
>
> Wondrously strange was earth to see,
> Flowers white as milk did gleam;
> Spread to Heaven the Assyrian Tree,
> Over my head with Dream.

Dews were still betwixt us twain;
Stars a trembling beauty shed;
Yet—not a whisper comes again
Of the words he said.

This might be a deliberate description of the poet's communion with his reader. The poem is the type of his maturer work. He is even consistent enough to view as unreal the most hideous reality of the century—the War.

Mr. de la Mare's most vital mood, however, dates back to 1906 when his second book, *Poems*, appeared. His ultimate attitude is foreshadowed in the opening poem.

The loveliest thing on earth a shadow hath,
A dark and livelong hint of death,
Haunting it ever till its last faint breath.

This, the epitome of his latest and most pregnant spirit, that characteristic melancholy which permeates all his finest work, is stated continually throughout this early volume which is conceived on infinitely more serious lines than the bulk of his work in *Peacock Pie* and *The Listeners*. Many of the realizations that are

126

ultimately sealed in *The Veil* are quietly hinted
in poems like "Keep Innocency," and "Where is
thy Victory?";

> Life is a mockery if death
> Have the least power men say it hath . . .

and innumerable others, notably "The Universe" and the sonnet "Humanity" with its
magnificent simile of the bird's cry and its awful
realization of time's eternity—

> Then stooped our manhood nearer, deep and still,
> As from earth's mountains an unvoyaged sea,
> Hushed my faint voice in its great peace until
> It seemed but a bird's cry in eternity;
> And in its future loomed the undreamable,
> And in its past slept simple men like me.

This, and the accompanying poems, link up at
every point with Mr. de la Mare's most recent
poetry and it is certainly no mere coincidence
that, in the two volumes of his collected works,
he has reprinted *Poems* in the same volume as
The Listeners and *Motley*, although by chronological rights it should have accompanied *Songs*

of Childhood which is bound with *Peacock Pie* in the other volume.

Thus the bulk of his really thoughtful work appears in *Poems, Motley,* and again particularly in *The Veil* where the melancholy mood turns grim. These books include very few of his children's poems. He is increasingly concerned with those "dark and livelong hints of death" mentioned in a previous quotation. Beauty, in the words of another poem, has

> . . . a thousand cheating names,
> But none foretokens rest.

Transcience, age, decay, mortality, always the trouble and despair of the philosophic poet observing mankind and nature, are the chief preoccupations of his subsequent work. But this deepening of his mood does not immediately disturb the glamorous surface of his poetry. In *Peacock Pie* his famous double-edged "Song of the Mad Prince" is still superficially a nursery rhyme, the neighbour of innocent little lyrics like "The Bandog" and "Miss T."

128

Who said, "Peacock Pie"?
  The old King to the sparrow:
Who said: "Crops are ripe"?
  Rust to the harrow:
Who said, "Where sleeps she now?
  Where rests she now her head,
Bathed in Eve's loveliness"?
  That's what I said.

Who said, "Ay, mum's the word"?
  Sexton to willow:
Who said, "Green dust for dreams,
  Moss for a pillow"?
Who said, "All Time's delight
  Hath she for narrow bed;
Life's troubled bubble broken"?
  That's what I said.

There is method in this kind of madness, though
it defies close analysis. The simplicity is only
superficial. To a child this poem may be nothing more than a delightful nursery rhyme. But
the older and more sophisticated reader cannot
escape hearing through the quietly chiming
verse the haunting *cri du cœur* that is repeated

in many a poignant variation of baffled thought
and intense feeling ever and again throughout
the poet's work. Even a stupid or insensitive
person, deaf to this sound and asking no more
of verse than its apparent surface charms of
rhythm and rhyme, may still, like the child, find
everything here to surprise and delight him.
But, little by little, this concern for "life's troubled bubble" increases as the poet's work de-
velops. The true de la Mare is gradually
revealed as a brooding, melancholy spirit,
puzzled and bewildered by the quarreling claims
of reality and unreality, and attempting to reconcile things imagined or dreamed or desired
with things accepted or known. Like Don Juan
in Flecker's play he is "a spirit troubled about
departure." His metaphysical speculations are
so unsatisfactory as to throw him back upon
the most beautiful aspects of reality in his effort to interpret the significance of the shadow
of even the loveliest thing on earth. He tries
to comfort himself with the realization of
beauty.

Leave this vain questioning. Is not sweet the rose?
Sings not the wild bird ere to rest he goes?
Hath not in miracle brave June returned?
Burns not her beauty as of old it burned?
   O foolish one to roam
So far from thine own mind away from home.

This is the poetry of escape. But the comfort
is only temporary. He cannot quiet his intellect and in the end we are confronted with
such a beautiful but terrible poem as is dic-
tated by his essential philosophy, the poem
"Futility" from *The Veil.*

   Sink, thou strange heart, unto thy rest.
     Pine now no more, to pine in vain,
  Doth not the moon on heaven's breast
     Call the floods home again?

   Doth not the summer faint at last?
     Do not her restless rivers flow
  When that their transient day is past
     To hide them in ice and snow?

  All this—thy world—an end shall make,
     Planet to sun return again,

The universe, to sleep from wake,
   In a last peace remain.

Alas! the futility of care
That, spinning thought to thought, doth weave
An idle argument on the air
   We love not or believe.

This, in fact, may be taken as a typical later utterance of this poet, who, by some strange irony, is best known today as the author of fanciful children's verses, distinguished for their candid innocence and delicate music. But in prose and verse alike (his poetry belongs to both) Mr. de la Mare's melancholy, stripped of its many disguises, is a match for anything in Thomas Hardy or Mr. A. E. Housman in their most pessimistic moods. Not all the cloud cap't towers and gorgeous palaces of his imagination can quite obscure the dark horizons of his view in the two later volumes, *Motley* and *The Veil*. The very titles bear witness to the mood. The note of futility sounds deeper and stronger. Even those poems wherein he most seeks to escape from the apparent conclusions of his philos-

ophy are touched by some sense of hopelessness.
The symbolism already observed in "The Song
of the Mad Prince" crystallizes subsequently in
such poems as "The Old Angler" and "The
Moth"—

> Isled in the midnight air,
>   Musked in the dark's faint bloom,
> Out into glooming and secret haunts
>   The flame cries, "Come!"
>
> Lovely in dye and fan,
>   A-tremble in shimmering grace,
> A moth from her winter swoon
>   Uplifts her face.
>
> Stares from her glamorous eyes;
>   Wafts her on plumes like mist;
> In ecstasy swirls and sways
>   To her strange tryst.

As before, if we are concerned only with the
literal meaning of the poem we shall not find
complete contact with the author's imagination.
It would be difficult to find another theme so
grim and remorseless as this. Deceived by the

rare colours and contours of the verse, the casual
reader will fail to realize the larger significance,
larger even, perhaps, than Shelley's

> . . . devotion to something afar
> From the sphere of our sorrow.

But to consider "The Tryst" with reference to
the poet's dominating mood is to enter upon
a new realization of his poetic character. In
his most recent work Mr. de la Mare has dotted
his *I*'s and crossed his *T*'s less than ever. Without sacrificing the interest of his less intellectual
reader he requires subtler realizations than of
old. Sooner or later, of course, his symbols
will compel recognition. In the meantime it is
a considerable proof of his poetic genius that
his poems can continue to exist as poems quite
apart from their deepest significance.

Nevertheless, in spite of these major considerations, it would be gross folly to pass over
his earlier, less important poems, as slight or
insufficient. Even in his merest nursery rhyming Mr. de la Mare's idiom is individual and
unmistakable. If he had never risen any higher

134

than such things as "The Bandog" we should
still be deeply in his debt.

> Has anybody seen my Mopser?
>   A comely dog is he,
> With hair of the colour of a Charles the Fifth
>   And teeth like ships at sea,
> His hair it curls straight upwards,
>   His ears stand two abreast,
> And he answers to the simple name of Mopser,
>   When civilly addressed.

But it is a far cry from this to such things as
"The Listeners" and "Arabia," "The Ghost,"
and "All That's Past," his loveliest lyric with
its wonderful opening stanza, epitomizing all
that poetry has said or can say concerning Time:

> Very old are the woods;
>   And the buds that break
> Out of the brier's boughs
>   When March winds wake,
> So old in their beauty are—
>   Oh, no man knows
> Through what wild centuries
>   Roves back the rose.

135

This, indeed, is to say what has oft been said before "but ne'er so well expressed." It is also a capital instance of the ancient truth that no theme is too old for new poetic treatment provided that the poet has an idiom of his own with which to express it.

Mr. de la Mare found his idiom during the years immediately preceding the war. The verse wherein he has employed it to the best effect is, however, insufficiently known. Thus it will be well to examine some aspects of his artistry which might not too easily be overlooked. Like all good poets he has long realized that the best poetry is achieved by means of a rapid succession of slight surprises. At each new turn the reader's interest must be refreshed by the occurrence of some unexpected inevitability. Mr. de la Mare is a cunning master of this particular power. He achieves his effects by constantly changing means. In one place the surprise is created by a characteristic trick that adds or drops a stressed syllable in some unexpected place in the verse. Or, it may be, without offending the actual pattern of the

136

verse, he will suddenly change his vital stresses
in complete but delightful defiance of the reader's anticipations. Contrast some stanzas from
"Alexander" where the changes are particularly
obvious.

It was the great Alexander,
　　Capped with a golden helm,
Sate in the ages, in his floating ship,
　　In a dead calm.

　　　*　　*　　*　　*　　*

Like a bold boy sate their Captain,
　　His glamour withered and gone,
In the songs of his brooding mariners,
　　While the song pined on.

　　　*　　*　　*　　*　　*

Come the calm, infinite night,
　　Who then will hear
Aught save the singing
　　Of the sea-maids clear?

This is nothing less than a fine extension of the
method employed by Coleridge in "Christabel,"
that scansion by stress instead of by syllable
wherein lies the true compromise between strict

metre and free verse. (It may best be noted now that Mr. de la Mare's honorable debt to Coleridge does not cease here. We may trace the influence again in the atmospheric character of various poems—notably "Arabia"—where he has recaptured that glamorous, dream-lulled world once peculiar to "Kubla Khan" and later recaptured by Poe.) And sometimes Mr. de la Mare will create his surprise by a deliberate lapse into tortuous phraseology or unusually bold inversion. In the whole range of poetry it would perhaps be impossible to find an instance of inversion so multiplied as in his line— "Pictured once her image I, sang gliding brook its rushes from. . . . " But what a loss of music and meaning if this be paraphrased. "The gliding brook sang from its rushes, 'I once pictured her image.' " The spell has been completely broken. If the line were not good poetry there would be no offense in the paraphrase. Instead we have substituted a plain statement of fact for the sound of a brook murmuring in its reeds. Mr. de la Mare's tortuousness is not always a matter of thought for

138

verbal inversion. His metrical patterns are
often unusually complex quite apart from the
considerations just suggested. "The Galliass"
may be cited not only as an instance of his ingenious metrical craft but also because it provides an outstanding example of his richest
symbolism. No other living poet presses so
many archaic and unusual words into his service. But there is seldom any suspicion of affectation or preciosity in their poetic use. They
are always something more than mere ornament.

"Tell me, tell me
   Unknown stranger
When shall I sight me
   That tall ship
On whose flower-wreathed counter is gilded *Sleep?*"

"Landsman, landsman,
   Lynx nor kestrel
Ne'er shall descry from
   Ocean steep
That midnight-stealing, high-pooped galliass *Sleep.*"

"Promise me, Stranger,
   Though I mark not

139

When cold night-tide's
  Shadows creep
Thou wilt keep unwavering watch for *Sleep*."

"Myriad the lights are,
  Wayworn landsman,
Rocking the dark through
  On the deep:
She alone burns none to prove her *Sleep*."

At first sight the poem may appear crabbed and writhen. But once accustomed to the unfamiliar arrangement and curious music of the lapping phrase so cunningly superimposed upon the metrical pattern (the poem should be read aloud) even a suspicious reader must admit an artistic success. These, then, are some notable devices whereby Mr. de la Mare has evolved his original, complicated technique, the poetic style which stamps everything he writes with his own peculiar idiom, the style that cannot be mistaken for another man's. This, with the character of his imagination already noticed, has made him the enigmatical figure among the poets of today.

140

JOHN MASEFIELD

John Masefield

THE publication of Mr. Masefield's "Everlasting Mercy" two years before the war marked a period in the history of modern poetry. The immediate and sweeping success of that poem not only sowed the seed of a harvest of public interest which was subsequently reaped by Mr. Edward Marsh and other anthologists of the rising poets, but it also popularized the reaction against a thin and spiritless type of verse that had survived Edwardian times from the late nineties. Mr. Rudyard Kipling, Mr. Alfred Noyes, and Sir Henry Newbolt, not to mention Mr. Masefield himself (in *Salt Water Ballads*) had already begun to substitute something in the nature of "guts and blood" for the "pale lost lilies" of Ernest Dowson and his immediate contemporaries. Several of the younger poets were swift to seize and even to exaggerate the example. Among others Rupert Brooke departed from his characteristic manner to write "Menelaus and Helen."

Hot through Troy's ruin Menelaus broke
To Priam's palace, sword in hand, to sate
On that adulterous whore a ten year's hate
And a king's honour. . . .

Again in "A Channel Passage" he went as far
as the violences of realism could take him.

Retchings twist and tie me,
Old meat, good meals, brown gobbets, up I throw.
Do I remember? Acrid return and slimy,
The sobs and slobber of a last year's woe.
And still the sick ship rolls. 'Tis hard I tell ye,
To choose twixt love and nausea, heart and belly.

He and many of those younger poets, destined
soon to be grouped together under that decep-
tive label "Georgian," were already known to
an absurdly small number of readers who
bravely attempted to keep in touch with current
poetry. But the general public (although they
were reading Mr. Kipling and Mr. Noyes)
knew little and cared less about the work of
the growing generation of poets until its curi-
osity was shocked by the publication of "The
Everlasting Mercy" in *The English Review.*

Mr. Masefield called a new tune which set the muse dancing, not very classically, in full view of the man in the street for the first time since the days of Tennyson. The subsequent outbreak of war coupled with the interest created by the romantic death of Rupert Brooke completed the victory over public apathy. For several years poetry competed with the novel for popular favour. In the end, of course, poetry lost the battle. But during those years new reputations were made, not least the reputation of Mr. Masefield himself.

He had been instrumental in guiding English verse back to virility again after a long period of comparative effeminacy and decadence. The poets themselves had driven the common reader away from verse, as so many of them have done in more recent times. Mr. Masefield brought the common reader back to poetry. All this, however, is not merely to say that he re-introduced violence, crude realism, and bad language into English verse. There is no special virtue in such a typical passage of his earlier work as—

145

"You closhy put."
"You bloody liar."
"This is my field."
"This is my wire."
"I'm ruler here."
"You ain't."
"I am."
"I'll fight you for it."
"Right, by damn."

Taken as they stand such things are merely crude and sordid, easy transcriptions of actuality that scarcely make any pretence of art. But they were, nevertheless, the immediately arresting signs of a more valid forcefulness which lay behind less noisy passages of "The Everlasting Mercy" and the subsequent narrative poems.

Down in the lane so thin and dark,
The tan-yards stank of bitter bark,
The curate's pigeons gave a flutter,
A cat went courting down the gutter,
And none else stirred a foot or feather,
The houses put their heads together,
Talking, perhaps, so dark and sly,

146

Of all the folk they'd seen go by,
Children, and men and women, merry all,
Who'd some day pass that way for burial.

Neither quotation could be offered as a specimen of impressive poetry, though, in their respective contexts, both are effective.

Mr. Masefield's method is not very common in modern verse, and at no time in the past has it achieved poetry of any really high order. In his narrative works no particular line is ever so good as to shine brighter than its immediate neighbours. Even in those passages where he rises into one of those intermittent bursts of poetry which occur throughout his pages, the lines are set at a dead level of quality which they sustain without much rise or fall till the burst ends.

I opened window wide and leaned
Out of that pigstye of the fiend
And felt a cool wind go like grace
About the sleeping market place.
The clock struck three, and sweetly, slowly,
The bells chimed, Holy, Holy, Holy;

147

And in a second's pause there fell
The cold note of the chapel bell,
And then a cock crew, flapping wings,
And summat made me think of things.
How long those ticking clocks had gone
From church and chapel, on and on,
Ticking the time out, ticking slow
To men and girls who'd come and go,
And how they ticked in belfry dark
When half the town was bishop's park,
And how they'd rung a chime full tilt
The night after the church was built,
And how that night was Lambert's Feast,
The night I'd fought and been a beast.

It is apparent here that he only seeks to achieve cumulative effects, relying on the sheer vigour and speed of his verse to distract the reader's attention from the coarseness of its poetic texture. In these long poems he seldom writes an immediately arresting line or phrase. On the whole, their verse is verbally and rhythmically clumsy and beats with a metronomic regularity that permits little variation within the time pattern. His style is a negative quality. His com-

148

mand of language is characteristically lusty and crude; his verbal music always harsh, and its colours florid. One might search his collected poems for hours before finding a music less coarse than that of his over-tearful lyric "The West Wind."

It's a warm wind, the west wind, full of bird's cries;
I never hear the west wind but the tears are in my
    eyes.
For it comes from the west land, the old brown hills,
And April's in the west wind, and daffodils.

It's a fine land, the west land, for hearts as tired as
    mine,
Apple orchards blossom there, and the air's like wine.
There is cool green grass there, where men may lie
    at rest,
And the thrushes are in song there, fluting from the
    nest.

Here too, incidentally, is a fairly naked specimen of the poet's frequent sentimental mood. The feeling is as coarse as the music; as for thought, there is merely the necessary minimum. The same kind of mushiness occurs throughout

149

the narrative poems, notably in "The Daffodil Fields," a poem which, nevertheless, contains some of his most eloquent passages. But the mushiness is unforgiveable.

Michael, my own heart's darling, speak; it's me
Mary. You know my voice. I'm here, dear, here.
Oh, little golden-haired one, listen. See,
It's Mary, Michael. Speak to Mary, dear.
Oh, Michael, little love, he cannot hear;
And you have killed him, Lion; he is dead.
My little friend, my love, my Michael, golden head.

Ugh! One remembers with a shudder "my little white vlower" in "The Tragedy of Nan." Mr. Masefield can be grossly sentimental.

In all the preceding quotations, as in all his earlier poems, and even in his later and finest work, we may observe a certain coa.seness of texture extending beyond the surface limits of language and theme. This proceeds partly from his rough-and-ready imagination, and partly from his technical limitations, which, for so good a poet, are undeniably considerable. Despite his narrative power and the rather urgent themes of all his longer poems, themes requiring a fairly loose verse-structure, the lines recurrently incline to fall into something less than the jingling kind of verse which may have been necessary in many places. A certain amount of looseness (though not so much as Mr. Masefield permits himself) may be expected in the style of any narrative poet who engages in the ancient battle with realism. It is impossible for his long poems not to sag sometimes. But if one complains of Mr. Masefield's failing in this respect it is not so much because his poems sag as because they frequently do so unnecessarily. The most prolific authors are, in general, the most careless craftsmen. Mr. Masefield, one of the most prolific poets of our time, is no exception to this rule. Haste and carelessness in workmanship leave their marks all over his collected works. He has never learned the whole lesson of poetic economy.

But he counterbalances these defects (so far as they can be counterbalanced) by the sheer muscle and sinew which give vitality to his verse as a whole. Primarily a teller of stories—for

151

even in his later lyrics he frequently takes the
rôle of story-teller—he has made it his chief
business to accelerate the movement of whatever narrative he has in hand. Because of its
haste and eagerness his verse constantly strag-
gles into doggerel. These very lapses, occurring
as they do almost side by side with his finer
passages, help by contrast to strengthen his outbursts. But there is no excuse for the doggerel.
Even at its best this method of approaching
the poetic climax is expensive. After many
repetitions the reader begins to resent what is
an obviously mechanical trick. All poetry, of
course, is in one sense trickery; but interest
ceases once the trickery becomes apparent. Excepting the "Dauber," Mr. Masefield's early
narratives (and even so late a work as "King
Cole") are frequently marred by the overin-
dulgence of this sleight. The key of the verse
is switched too suddenly and too often from one
extreme of expression to the other. Only rarely
is there a gradual transition. A specimen of
Mr. Masefield's over-rapid leaps from one kind

of verse to another may be quoted from "The Widow in the Bye Street."

Man cannot call the brimming instant back;
Time's an affair of instants spun to days;
If man must make an instant gold, or black,
Let him, he may, but time must go his ways.
Life may be duller for an instant's blaze.
Life's an affair of instants spun to years,
Instants are only cause of all these tears.

Then Anna screamed aloud. "Help. Murder. Mur-
   der."
"By God it is," he said. "Through you, you slut."
Backing she screamed until the blacksmith heard her.
"Hurry," they cried, "the woman's throat's being
   cut."
"He might come to," he said, "with wine or soup.
"I only hit him once, like, with the scoop."

The anticlimax is even more startling in passages where the poet suddenly springs from such unnecessarily broad realism as appears in the second of these stanzas into some sudden purple passage describing, say, a sunset or the landscape.

153

These discords are rarely resolved in Mr. Masefield's work. In his earlier work he never discovered the right pitch for his instrument. Thus the parodists have been swift to recognize and stab at the most vulnerable slits in his poetic armour, and it is impossible not to admit the fairness of their criticism. The narrative method of "The Everlasting Mercy," "The Widow in the Bye Street," and "The Daffodil Fields" can be traced most easily, particularly as regards its weaknesses, in Mr. Masefield's curious little tale of Farmer Kyrle, who used to beat his daughter after market. Here we meet another sordid story told without any attempt to avoid the poet's characteristic shock tactics. But to what end?

> Young Will, the son,
> Heard his sister shriek;
> He took his gun
> Quick as a streak.
>
> He said: "Now, dad,
> Stop, once for all!"

154

JOHN MASEFIELD

He was a good lad,
Good at kicking the ball.

His father clubbed
The girl on the head.
Young Will upped
And shot him dead.

"Now sister," said Will,
"I've a-killed father,
As I said I'd kill.
O my love, I'd rather

"A-kill him again
Than see you suffer.
O my little Jane
Kiss goodbye to your brother.

"I won't see you again,
Nor the cows homing,
Nor the mice in the grain,
Nor the primrose coming."

    *   *   *   *   *

They hanged Will,
As Will said;

155

With one thrill
They choked him dead.

Here, in miniature, we see Mr. Masefield's method, with some of its virtues and all its shortcomings; his power of rising into poetry, though too suddenly, by the trick of contrast, in the penultimate stanza; in the second, his unbelievable bathos; in the fourth and fifth, his false simplicity; and throughout all the verses, his determination to get on with the story at all costs, a virtue that cannot be over-praised. All these examples can be matched in the longer poems.

But, one may ask, what particularly is the value of these ultra-realistic accounts in verse of people and crimes so sordid that even the most unpleasant police court records can rarely match them? It would not be true to say that Mr. Masefield raises them to the level of tragedy, like other poets who have chosen parallel themes. He is not even particularly interested in the psychological aspects of his characters. Certainly the bare tales have no special value in themselves. Yet, with the exception of an occasional rhapsodic outburst, usually in praise of the landscape, and intermittent platitudinous side-comments like the "Man cannot bring the brimming moment back," quoted above, Mr. Masefield adds nothing to relieve his unyielding realism. He is content merely to tell a crude story in crude and hasty verse, apparently for its own sake. But to what end?—for that can scarcely be accepted as a sufficient explanation of the author's purpose. He would not, I think, be the man to subscribe to any "art for art's sake" explanation of his poetic motives. In any case such an explanation would not be very acceptable to the puzzled reader of the stanzas about Farmer Kyrle and Young Will, not to mention "The Daffodil Fields" and "The Widow in the Bye Street." It may be that these poems, like "The Everlasting° Mercy," are intended to serve some moral purpose. If so, it is only very vaguely implied. In the end Mr. Masefield's intention remains in doubt and it is not altogether unfair to regard these poems as so many interesting exercises in narrative verse, remarkable chiefly for their perverse insistence on ugliness and evil.

One other characteristic weakness may be noted before passing on to Mr. Masefield's compensating virtues. It can best be described as a confusion regarding the true nature of simplicity. This, primarily, is an attitude of the mind, not a mere matter of subject-matter and language. Words and meter by themselves cannot translate simplicity out of life into poetry. The compromise between pure realism and ordinary speech is one of the most difficult problems of poetry. And however much we may theorize about it, the most successful poetic practice has shown that the language of everyday life (especially when it is the everyday life of people like Saul Kane and Jimmy Gurney) is not the language of poetry until it has been rearranged and rarefied. In short, unless poetry is to be sacrificed to prosaic realism, it is necessary to modify such language as would be employed by a real Saul Kane until its poetic equivalent has been found. To do this without passing to the

opposite extreme of poetic diction is not easy.
Wordsworth and Hardy, the authors of some
of the simplest poetry falling in this category,
both poets of exceptional intellectual power and
masters of poetic technique, struggled unceas-
ingly with this same problem which Mr. Masefield has never successfully solved. We need
look no farther than the poem last quoted for
a typical example of his failure to make the
necessary approximation. His realism smothers
the poetry, chiefly because he conceives simplicity as a mere matter of words. He gives
us, as it were, a verbal photograph of an actual
event, instead of translating a spiritual experience into words.

These defects, however, belong mainly to his
earlier narrative poems. In the whole length
of "Reynard the Fox," his masterpiece, there
is scarcely a false note. That this should be
so suggests that he is a poet whose success is
governed chiefly by his subject-matter. For in
the later poem, "King Cole," many of the
former shortcomings reappear. Again, in
"Philip the King" and "Good Friday," dramatic

poems written in dialogue, we recognize the same uncertainty of characterization that may be noticed in "The Everlasting Mercy." Pilate, in one play, speaks in a voice indistinguishable from that of Philip in the other. Such technical devices as the particular form supplies are not sufficiently in the author's command. He cannot speak from inside his characters. They are nothing more than two names for his own voice.

But in "The Dauber" and "Reynard" Mr. Masefield gives us the rarest of his presents, really long outbursts of beautiful, vivid poetry uninterrupted by the clamors and banalities of his more raucous Muse. There is little in the story of either of these poems to encourage new expeditions into sordidness. They contain no such gratuitous realism as may be found in the earlier works—

> The dawn finds them filling empty cans
> In some sweet-smelling, dusty country lane
> Where a brook chatters over rusty pans.

Mr. Masefield is always at his best when he

sets out to describe men in the heat of action.
All his love of reality (not realism) and movement are poured out in these two poems. In
"The Everlasting Mercy" nothing surpassed the
description of the fight at the beginning of the
poem. Even this, however, is inferior to the
magnificent account of the Dauber's voyage
round Cape Horn. Here, happy in his mood
as in his subject-matter, Mr. Masefield gives
free rein to his genius and leaves criticism gasp-
ing for breath.

> Two hours passed, then a dim lightening came.
> Those frozen ones upon the yard could see
> The mainsail and the foresail still the same.
> Still battling with the hands and blowing free,
> Rags tattered where the staysails used to be.
> The lower topsails stood; the ship's lee deck
> Seethed with four feet of water filled with wreck.

From here onward the crescendo is firm, gradual, sure—a triumph of poetic government.
The ensuing storm is described with all the same
force and gusto which the author used later
when he followed the Ghost Heath Run in

"Reynard." Even Joseph Conrad, that master of poetic prose, in spite of his greater sea-knowledge, when he described in "Typhoon" another of the great storms of literature wrote little better. And the Dauber himself is a real character whose every word and action carries a conviction foreign to Saul Kane or Jimmy Gurney or the characters in "The Daffodil Fields," where the story again forces the poet to commit coarse violences in the midst of some of his loveliest descriptions of the English countryside.

Again in "Reynard," written and published some six years later, after various excursions into the drama and some notable achievements in the sonnet form, Mr. Masefield, definitely modelling his poem on Chaucerian lines, surpassed the best of his former work. All the sounds and sights of the typical English meet, set in the loveliest countryside, are imbedded in his rapidly moving, sketchy verse.

> The stables were alive with din
> From dawn until the time of meeting.
> A pad-groom gave a cloth a beating,

Knocking the dust out with a stake.
Two men cleaned stalls with fork and rake
And one went whistling to the pump,
The handle whined ker-lump, ker-lump,
The water splashed into the pail,
And, as it went, it left a trail. . . .

The poem opens with a catalogue of characters which compares very favorably with the Chaucerian prologue from which it patently derives. But Mr. Masefield is no slavish imitator. If he takes the ready-made pattern, it is not because he lacks matter and originality to weave it in his own way. The fox has even more character than the men and women who ride to the hunt, more than

> Molly Wolveset, riding straddle,
> Red as a rose, with eyes like sparks.

More even than the Parson:

> His jolly eyes were bright with fun.
> His jolly mouth was well inclined
> To cry aloud his jolly mind
> To everyone in jolly terms.

163

He did not talk of churchyard worms,
But of our privilege as dust
To box a lively bout with lust
Ere going to Heaven to rejoice.

There is no more exciting story in modern literature than the story of the Ghost Heath Run. Here at last the poet has achieved realism without sacrificing poetry by the way. He ensnares all our sympathies for Reynard without antagonizing us against the hunters. It was a cunning inspiration to introduce a second fox to cross the scent and divert the pack from its original quarry before the end of the chase. When the death cry begins the excitement rises to fever heat and the reader is too delighted by the escape of Reynard to spare many of his sympathies for the less fortunate animal. He forgets that Peter has been robbed to pay Paul.

At the close of this most thrilling poem we can pause to bask for a while in the full sun of poetic propriety (one might almost say "poetic justice"). Reynard, after the hardest run of his life, has found cover at last.

And the hunt came home and the hounds were fed,
They climbed to their bench and went to bed,
The horses in stable loved their straw.
"Goodnight, my beauties," said Robin Dawe.
Then the moon came quiet and flooded full
Light and beauty on clouds like wool,
On a feasted fox at rest from hunting,
In the beech-wood grey where the brocks were
    grunting.
The beech-wood grey rose dim in the night
With moonlight fallen in pools of light,
The long dead leaves on the ground were rimed.
A clock struck twelve and the church-bells chimed.

So ends one of the most remarkable poems in modern literature.

At the side of "Reynard" all but his finest lyrics and sonnets seem thin and pale. They have less of that grip and verve, that keen and nervous virility which makes every line in this poem contribute its full quota to the whole effect. "Reynard" never sinks into doggerel. There is no superfluity, no objectionable violence for its own sake (in spite of a certain violence in the actual subject), no sentimental

strain such as stales his *Salt Water Ballads*. His
joy in the speed and pageant of the hunt and
in the panorama of the landscape never fails
him. It is the same whenever he is writing
about wholesome action. The fight in "The
Everlasting Mercy," the boat race in "Biography," his sonnet "The Racer"—

I saw the racer coming to the jump,
  Staring with fiery eyeballs as he rusht,
I heard the blood within his body thump,
  I saw him launch, I heard the toppings crusht.

And as he landed I beheld his soul
  Kindle, because, in front, he saw the Straight
With all its thousands roaring at the goal,
  He laughed, he took the moment for his mate.

Would that the passionate moods on which we ride
  Might kindle thus to oneness with the will
Would we might see the end to which we stride,
  And feel, not strain in struggle, only thrill.

And laugh like him and know in all our nerves
Beauty, the spirit scattering dust and turves.

—all these reveal his realism at its best and

even lend themselves, as here, to an allegorical idealization. When he chooses to describe squalid life, murder and sudden death, as in most of the earlier narratives, realism runs away with the poetry time and again. Thus criticism recurs to a fact already mentioned, the fact that Mr. Masefield, more than most of his contemporaries, is easily victimized by his subject-matter. Physical appearances move him chiefly, action, movement, sound, light, colour, everything that combines to make the catalogue in "Biography" one of his finest poems. His feeling is always superior to his thought; indeed, his verse is generally commonplace when it approaches the realms of intellectual speculation. Even the "Beauty" sonnets in *Lollingdon Downs* are chiefly remarkable for the pictures and images they evoke, and these are the same in kind as the pictures of "Biography," "Ships," "The Wanderer," and all the finest of his shorter poems.

Here the legion halted, here the ranks were broken,
And the men fell out to gather wood;

And the green wood smoked, and bitter words were
    spoken,
And the trumpets called to food.

And the sentry on the rampart saw the distance
    dying
In the smoke of distance blue and far,
And heard the curlew calling and the owl replying
As the night came cold with one star;

And thought of home beyond, over moorland, over
    marshes,
Over hills, over sea, across the plains, across the pass,
By a bright sea trodden by the ships of Tarshis,
The farm with cicadae in the grass.

And thought, as I; "Perhaps, I may be done with
    living
Tomorrow, when we fight. I shall see those souls
    no more.
O beloved souls, be beloved in forgiving
The deeds and the words that make me sore."

Even here, in one of his most convincing lyrics,
one may note a certain vagueness of purpose,
a scattering of the energy. This poem is sub-

stantially the same as Mr. A. E. Housman's
"On Wenlock Edge," which has already been
quoted in another essay in this book. It is a
liberal education in the ways and means of the
poet to compare one poem with the other. Mr.
Masefield's long-windedness, his squandering
method could not be more effectively revealed.
His whole poem is contained in four of Mr.
Housman's lines.

> Then, 'twas before my time, the Roman
> At yonder heaving hill would stare;
> The blood that warms an English yeoman,
> The thoughts that hurt him, they were there.

Mr. Masefield's command of the picturesque is
usually cunning enough to divert the reader's
notice from the most characteristic weakness of
his work, that is, its uncertainty of purpose. He
seldom seems quite sure of what he intends to
say and this lack of definite direction which mars
so many of his poems is intensified by his habit
of accepting the first convenient rhyme that occurs and permitting it to direct the surrounding
thought.

169

The blacksmith in his sparky forge
Beat on the white hot softness there;
Ever as he beat he sang an air
To keep the sparks out of his gorge.

There can be nothing but a rhyme-driven plea for the fourth line; and this is only a casual example of his weakness.

A last word concerning Mr. Masefield's realism. The poet himself has said in a recent preface, perhaps a little too apologetically in his own behalf, that poets "either strive towards a greater elaboration of artifice or for a greater closeness to reality." This seems to me to suggest a false antithesis. Surely one endeavor does not necessarily exclude the other. In any case, reality is not the same thing as realism. Here, I believe, is the source of so much confusion in the minds of most of our realists today. There is as much reality, for instance, in the quiet work of the Poet Laureate as we can find in Mr. Masefield's books; but Mr. Bridges is never what one would call a realistic poet. Moreover, the best of Mr. Masefield's own work is surely that in which his realism is directed not exclusively (as in most of his early work) towards the uglier realities, but in those poems like "Dauber," "Reynard," the beautiful stanzas to his mother, and most of the lyrics and sonnets in *Lollingdon Downs*. It will be to these, I think, that future anthologists will look when they come to take toll of the poet's work, and not to *Salt Water Ballads*, his earliest volume, in which the influence of Mr. Kipling and Mr. Yeats is paramount. The romantic, sentimental lyrics (like "Sea Fever" and "Cargoes," that colourful hotch-potch in which there is no finite verb) have been preferred by Mr. Masefield's own generation. But his most characteristic work has never been his best. Had it been he might never have enjoyed the popularity which has followed him since 1912.

THREE IRISH POETS

Three Irish Poets

UNLESS one forgets the original intentions of its leaders and prophets, the Celtic Literary Revival cannot be regarded as an unqualified success. Social and political conditions during the past two decades have not dealt kindly with all the ambitious dreams of Mr. W. B. Yeats and his comrades in art who, in their earlier days, planned not only to create a distinctively national literature rooted in the Celtic past, but also to produce an Irish audience worthy of such a literature. A nation conscious and proud of its living artists was altogether too brave a dream to be realized, even in Ireland. Nevertheless, literature has been created, though not perhaps the distinctively national literature its makers planned. The ambition was too great for a single generation of poets. Synge, Mr. Yeats, A. E., have all had imitators; but who are their successors, the men able to continue and enlarge the tradition? The Irish theatre, of course, cannot be called wholly dead while Mr. Sean O'Casey continues to write,

175

though chiefly for the English and American
stage. He, however, is the only notable play-
wright who has arisen from the ashes of Synge
and Lady Gregory, whose plays, with those of
Mr. Padraic Colum and the verse-drama of Mr.
Yeats himself, have been elbowed off the stage
into the libraries where, it appears, they are
likely to repose for an indefinite period. A few
new prosemen and poets have appeared since
1919; but those who are not merely aping the
work of their older compatriots seem to have
turned away from Ireland to follow alien traditions. Mr. James Joyce, in whom so many
high hopes once were rested, has taken his perverted and bewildering genius to thrive, or, it
may be, to decay, in very different fields from
those his elders ploughed. Others, like Mr.
Liam O'Flaherty, derive little or nothing from
the impetus of the national movement. Not
for the first time Irish individualism has defeated Irish nationalism. The best-laid schemes
of those who originated the literary movement
have gone agley.

It would be foolish and even a little ungrateful to recall today the details of those schemes. It is enough to insist that in the attempt to fulfil them, a body of fine literature has been and is still, fitfully, being created. Within the past five or six years we have at least two of the most astonishing prose works Ireland has ever produced, the work of Mr. James Stephens, who is gradually re-telling with inimitable art and grace the old legends of his country. His Deirdre is incomparably finer than Lady Gregory's, or the Deirdre of Synge in spite of the fact that Mr. Stephens has clad her beauty in a simple prose narrative. Even more recently he has added another to the bright array of his little but precious books of verse. Again, after a long silence, A. E. has produced a volume of poems no less admirable than his earlier works. And the youngest of the group, Mr. Padraic Colum, in his Connecticut home has never forsworn his Celtic Muse. Nor is Mr. Yeats so engrossed by his senatorial duties as to forget the claims of his art. As this appreciation goes to press a new volume of his poems is announced.

Nevertheless, the outstanding Irish poets of the pre-war decade are the same men who stand unchallenged today. Newcomers, like Mr. F. R. Higgins and Mr. Austin Clarke, both poets of merit, cannot survive comparison with the early comparable work of Mr. Yeats and A. E. The members of the old group are aging, and it seems that the Irish literary movement is threatened by a setting sun, though one may expect to hear some rare music before the close. Yet it is difficult to believe that the movement will not sooner or later be revived, though perhaps in a less pugnaciously nationalistic form. Is it possible to write the literature of one race in the language of another? Whatever may be the answer to that difficult question, it is a fact that these Irish poets did not find their largest, or even their most appreciative audience within the shores of their own country. The language in which they wrote tied them hand and foot, willy-nilly, to its own poetic literature. They created an Irish tradition within the walls of the English tradition. Nationally conscious

178

American authors are in much the same case. A language more or less common to two countries tends to abolish all but the broadest national distinctions in literature.

And yet, within certain limits, Irish poetry during the past twenty years has been informed by a spirit in many respects alien to the contemporaneous spirit of English poetry. This has been chiefly due to the dominating influence of Mr. Yeats' poetry, which, more than any other single factor, has determined the mood most generally associated with the whole movement. It is a mood of weariness, melancholy, spiritual and physical attrition.

Come away, the red lips whisper, all the world is
    waiting now,
'Tis the twilight of the ages and it's time to quit
    the plough.

The poetic instrument is muted, the colors of the landscape are dimmed. The poet sees the world melting in a gray mist, and that mist has been called the Celtic twilight. Mr. Yeats' play *The Shadowy Waters* is particularly saturated with it. So too are innumerable early lyrics of his.

O curlew, cry no more in the air,
Or only to the water in the West;
Because your crying brings to my mind
Passion-dimmed eyes, and long heavy hair
That was shaken out over my breast;
There is enough evil in the crying of the wind.

Brows are pale, hair dim, hands still; water is wan, fire pale, eyes dove-gray. There is something of this atmosphere in all the poetry of the movement, and even in the work of men like Ledwidge and that grievously neglected poet Herbert Trench, though neither was ever really a figure in the Celtic school. Trench's "Deirdre Wedded" is bathed in the light from its first line to its last. But less skilful imitators of Mr. Yeats arose to degrade his lovely artifice until, finally, as we shall see, he abandoned it with certain other characteristic peculiarities of his early work. In general, the Celtic twilight since then has served as a ready-made substitute for real poetic "atmosphere"

in the work of writers who found in it a decep-
tive disguise for the attenuated substance of
their verse. With them Mr. Yeats' genuine
invention became a mere empty formula, a stock
of ready epithets, vague and unpurposed. Mr.
J. C. Squire has parodied the "numerous Celts"
who falsely affected the manner.

There's a grey wind wails on the clover,
And grey hills, and mist around the hills,
And a far voice sighing a song that is over,
And my grey heart that a strange longing fills.

This is devastating criticism, no less than—

Seven dead men, Brigit,
Came from the sea;
And each with his strange eyes
Whispered to me.

The atmosphere in the poetry of A. E. superficially resembles that of Mr. Yeats, but it is
essentially different in its cause and quality. Mr.
George Russell's (that is, A. E.'s) sympathy
with the aims of the Irish literary movement
has been more theoretic than practical so far as
concerns his poetry. The vital mood underlying

his work actually has little in common with
the moods of his fellow poets. Where Mr.
Yeats and Mr. James Stephens have tended to
see the world in terms of Ireland, he has seen
Ireland relatively in terms of the world. He
has been concerned primarily with the types of
things while they delight to particularize, preferably with Irish examples. To put the matter crudely, Mr. Yeats sees his swans at Coole
and tells us so. His lake-isle is pinned down
to Innisfree. A. E. would have reduced them
respectively to swans anywhere and a lake-isle
nowhere. This is not to suggest that he fails
to make use of the Irish scene. On the contrary, it is the basis of much of his description.
But there is nothing exceptionally Irish in such
a typical passage as

Twilight, a blossom grey in shadowy valleys dwells:
Under the radiant dark the deep blue-tinted bells
In quietness re-image heaven within their blooms,
Sapphire and gold and mystery. What strange per-
    fumes
Out of what deeps arising, all the flower bells fling
Unknowing the enchanted odorous song they sing.

There is something here of the atmosphere that belongs notably to Shelley's poetry, a certain mistiness, an unreality; the poet is describing a world of his own which, though it may have some counterpart in this physical world, would not appear in the same way to any other eyes. In short, Mr. Yeats and Mr. Stephens see the landscape as it is, while A. E. sees it as it is not, bathed in something of "The light that never was on sea or land." His stress is laid on the feeling, the colour, the atmosphere, never on the concrete form. The resemblance to Shelley appears throughout this poet's work more in the kind of imagery and simile employed than in the philosophic significance of the ideas which are essentially Wordsworthian.

Only the humble stones have kept
Their morning starriness of purity
Immutable. Being unfallen they breathe
Only unfallen life; and with my cheek
Pressed to their roughness I had part regained
My morning starriness and made these songs
Half from the hidden world and half from this.

183

The attitude is even better expressed in the short lyric called "Dust."

> I heard them in their sadness say,
>   "The earth rebukes the thought of God;
> We are but embers wrapped in clay
>   A little nobler than the sod."
>
> But I have touched the lips of clay,
>   Mother, thy rudest sod to me
> Is thrilled with fire of hidden day
>   And haunted by all mystery.

A. E.'s poetry is none the worse because it springs from one of the oldest "mystic"—I prefer to say philosophic, if not actually scientific —realizations of a certain type of mind. Most of his lyrics are in the nature of variations on the same theme.

In his imagery he prefers a cloud to a rock, a rainbow to a rose; and even his rocks and roses are clouded over with mist and twilight. He sees everything through a veil and sees everything as a veil. All nature is symbolic and each particular stone or blade of grass is a miniature symbol of the whole. He does not make it into

a symbol: it already exists as such. The resulting dimness that surrounds his verse—it is never
the dimness of obscurity—is not to be confused
with the "Celtic twilight" of Mr. Yeats and
the Yeatsian imitators. It is the same quality
that Matthew Arnold hinted at in Shelley.

The fact is that A. E., as has already been
suggested, is first of all a mystic poet and only
incidentally an Irish poet. It would be almost
impossible, however, to find a poem in the
earlier books of Mr. Yeats that does not bear
some unmistakable mark of its author's nation-
ality. Even in his purer later poems there is
generally some curious turn of the phrase, some
trick of the Irish voice, that marks it out not
only as the work of the poet Yeats but also
as the work of Yeats, the Irishman. And this
in spite of the fact that he has gradually wrung
out of his poetic style every element that is
not the absolute essence of his own artistic
individuality. A. E. is less explicit in all
respects, though never more economical in artistic practice. The difference is determined, of
course, by the fact that A. E. is engaged in the

continual apprehension of abstract ideas, the mystic or philosophical meaning, the significance of the appearance of things, while Mr. Yeats, less concerned with transcendental perceptions, is essentially a poet of the intellectual imagination. He is not satisfied with his imaginative apprehensions; he must also comprehend them intellectually. A. E. begins by idealizing everything, but Mr. Yeats' idealizations are comparatively accidental and incidental. And this habit of mind whereby A. E. sees every natural phenomenon as a symbol of one thing—God—is, I repeat, typically Wordsworthian. At times it can very definitely be associated with the more transcendental thought of the Orient, but, at its best, the general view is well epitomized in the lines from Tintern Abbey—

> A motion and a spirit that impels
> All thinking things, all objects of all thought,
> And rolls through all things.

Thus A. E. appears as a poet whose work refers to a point of view, a point of view by no means original in its philosophic character, yet startlingly original by means of the poetic ways whereby it is presented.

In this sense Mr. Yeats has no particular view to present. He is a poet governed by innumerable moods of the conscious imagination, not by any deep realization of some philosophic conception or faith. Excepting such things as are fundamental to all good poetry his work has few of the characteristics usual among his contemporaries in England and Ireland. If he derives from any particular English poet it is from Blake, though he is a much superior artist in verse. The most striking aspect of his poetic growth is the Blake-like determination to free himself of all extraneous influences; and gradually, in the course of many laborious years of work at his art, he has achieved a poetic idiom, a personal style, so remarkably individual that criticism is tempted to clap its hands and leave the flower undissected. And this peculiarly individual tone of his poetry is not that of his most familiar, earlier work. Fifteen years ago lazy critics were writing him down as a mystic and a symbolist, usually because of the affectations that then characterized his typical work. He might have indulged in the worst kind of obscurantism and many would have accepted it, content not to understand its meaning because of a superficial pleasure to be taken in its ornaments and decorations.

Mr. Yeats never appeared so much the master of his art as in that comparatively unknown and neglected volume *The Wild Swans at Coole*. In his collected poems it stands out in poetic quality far beyond the other peaks of his achievement. These later poems make much less difficult reading than the poems of 1889; that is to say, their meaning is much more clearly defined, less ambiguous and less dependent on more or less esoteric allusions than before. But as they are also less immediately romantic, less glamorous, and do not fall back upon the old Celtic mythology so frequently, a reader of the earlier poems often tends to overlook their greater plasticity and depth. With the toning down of the old mythological allusive appeal much of the superficial fascination has disappeared. The essential poetry, however, has merely been driven inward. A characteristic poem from *The Wild Swans at Coole* is altogether purer in essence than one from *The Wind among the Reeds*. Take, for instance, "A Deep-sworn Vow"—

Others because you did not keep
That deep-sworn vow have been friends of mine;
Yet always when I look death in the face,
When I clamber to the heights of sleep,
Or when I grow excited with wine,
Suddenly I meet your face.

The new restraint, the quietness of the verse in this and most of his later work (see particularly the title poem of the volume), cannot deceive anybody but a reader insensitive to the nuances of language and rhythm to think that the old passion of the poet has waned. Actually it is stronger and more vital than ever. The poetry is chastened in the extreme. Its surface scarcely ripples, but in the crystal depths we recognize the essential lineaments of the old imagination that used so often to disguise itself in the property masks of the Irish movement.

189

Mr. Yeats has himself told how and why he for-
swore his original ornaments and took to the
naked verse of his recent work.

> I made my song a coat
> Covered with embroideries
> Out of old mythologies
> From heel to throat;
> But the fools caught it,
> Wore it in the world's eyes
> As though they'd wrought it.
> Song, let them take it
> For there's more enterprise
> In walking naked.

This shedding of the coat has given the modern
world of poetry its most original voice. Neither
Mr. Bridges, nor Mr. Housman, the Irish poet's
greatest compeers, has developed a more pierc-
ing individuality than this that has produced
such a poem as *The Wild Swans at Coole.*

> The trees are in their Autumn beauty,
> The woodland paths are dry,
> Under the October twilight the water
> Mirrors a still sky;

Upon the brimming water among the stones
Are nine and fifty swans.

The nineteenth Autumn has come upon me
Since I first made my count;
I saw, before I had well finished
All suddenly mount
And scatter wheeling in great broken rings
Upon their clamorous wings.

Here and generally throughout the same volume the poet achieves the maximum quality of
poetry with the minimum amount of apparent
effort. The tone of the verse is almost conver-
sational, and yet that "almost" contains the
whole difference between the quality of casual
conversation and the quality of great poetry.
The obtrusive symbolism has disappeared with
the strained allusions and the artificial mists of
the Celtic twilight. Nothing extraneous remains. It may be well to take the simplest instance of all, the poem "To a Squirrel at Kyle-
na-Gno"—

Come play with me;
Why should you run

Through the shaking tree
    As though I'd a gun
To strike you dead?
    When all I would do
Is to scratch your head
    And let you go.

There is more cunning contrivance here than in
any of his earlier poems. Throughout all this
later work the poet's meaning and rhythm
never falter; his language is diamond-like, cut
from the solid rock without a flaw. And the
impulse of the poems is no less spontaneous
and affecting than that of his most popular
poem, the anthologists' favorite, with the wonderful vowel play, "The Lake Isle of Innisfree." It is not to that poem, however, that
we must look for the essential Mr. W. B. Yeats
but in the altogether rarer poetry of the later
books. It would be a mistake to disparage such
excellent early work for the mere purpose of
attracting attention to what has followed. That,
needless to say, is far from my present intention. But it is the inevitable temporary fate
of every poet who has achieved a certain degree

of popularity to secure it by means of a single poem or a single book in such a way that his subsequent work is neglected or insufficiently appreciated. I have tried elsewhere to indicate how this same thing has happened to certain English contemporaries of Mr. Yeats. In his instance there is even less justification, for he is among the two or three poets who stand ahead of and apart from all who are writing today.

Mr. James Stephens' wonderful aptitude for prose-romance tends to distract attention from his no less important poetic gifts. Nobody has ever written simpler poetry. His work may be said scarcely to deal with ideas at all. A bird's song, the cry of a snared rabbit and the vital, overwhelming desire to release it, the crooked windings of a goat path on the side of a hill— these and such as these are his themes. He seeks only to convey the feeling of an experience, never to describe it in any realistic sense. And, rarest of attributes among the serious poets of today, he has a certain tint of humour that glitters on the edges of his happier moods with such a brightness as belongs only to poetry. It is often faintly ironical, not unlike the humour in "Deirdre" and "The Crock of Gold." This has given us the unique poetry of "Peadar Og Goes Courting" and "The Merry Policeman," to say nothing of such a remarkable poem as "The Sootherer." But the best of Mr. Stephens is to be found in those intense and passionate poems of his sympathy which relate his work so closely with that of the English poet, Mr. Ralph Hodgson, such things as "The Snare"—

> I heard a sudden cry of pain!
> There is a rabbit in a snare:
> Now I hear the cry again,
> But I cannot tell from where.
>
> But I cannot tell from where
> He is calling out for aid;
> Crying on the frightened air,
> Making everything afraid.
>
> Making everything afraid,
> Wrinkling up his little face,
> As he cried again for aid;
> And I cannot find the place.

And I cannot find the place
  Where his paw is in the snare:
Little one! Oh, little one!
  I am searching everywhere.

The same keen intensity characterizes his gayer
moods. He will take a mere phrase and turn
it inside out and round about in unfailing poetry.
In terms of reason and argument he seems to
be saying scarcely anything at all. But between
the lines he can convey the meaning of his mood,
the sense of an experience, no less clearly than
Alexander Pope could make the epigrammatic
statement gleam through his rigid couplet:

I heard a bird at dawn
  Singing sweetly on a tree,
That the dew was on the lawn
  And the wind was on the lea,
But I didn't listen to him
  For he didn't sing to me.

In a further two stanzas that do little more than
vary the order of these phrases he evokes all
the sounds and smells and feelings of a breezy
summer day. He makes his own song vie with

that of the bird. The matter is slight enough; not so the mood. Mr. Stephens has definite limitations, but they are the limitations of a fairy. He is an elf among the modern poets.

ALFRED NOYES

Alfred Noyes

MR. ALFRED NOYES has generally been associated, at least in name, with Mr. Rudyard Kipling and Sir Henry Newbolt in the so-called "imperialistic" school of modern English poetry, and thus, although he is not yet fifty, it is very easy to think of him as one of the older poets. His first volume of verse, *The Loom of Years*, was published originally in 1902, the same year as Mr. Masefield's *Salt Water Ballads*. Since then Mr. Noyes has maintained an output of work larger than that of almost any other poet of our day. By the time his ambitious "Drake" appeared, in 1906, fairly soon after the poet's graduation from Oxford, the reviewers were beginning to refer to him as if to a new Tennyson, one who had come to address the age with such a poetry as would simultaneously delight the great mass of verse readers and yet win the approval of the literati of the time. His popularity was almost instantaneous, and it is still more of a reality with the common reader both

199

in England and America than might be sus-
pected by a casual observer.

In England, then, there still existed a fairly
large public with a fondness for straightforward, singing verse, the more highly-coloured
the better. Mr. Kipling had kept this public
alive with very little help from elsewhere before Mr. Noyes came to join him. The new
poet's work was in the broad tradition and de-
rived not unpleasantly from poetry already
known and accepted by the mass of people, who
naturally welcomed it. Mr. Noyes had not discovered any particular idiom of his own with
which to match Mr. Kipling's individual voice;
but his choice of poetic material was generally
acceptable, pleasant, appealing, full of crude
movement, good stories, whispers of fairyland,
coarse music and romantic colours. He wrote
"poetic" poetry; he was not afraid of rhetoric.
While Mr. Bridges was still caviare to the general Mr. Noyes captivated the popular imagination with such idle jingles as the famous "Barrel
Organ."

Come down to Kew in lilac-time,
   In lilac-time, in lilac-time,
Come down to Kew in lilac-time,
   It isn't far from London.
And we will wander hand in hand
   With love in summer's wonderland,
Come down to Kew in lilac-time,
   It isn't far from London.

This bagatelle was no better and no worse than it pretended to be. But it was not poetry and the critics who hailed it as such did no good service to the future reputation of the author.

"Drake" with its pseudo-epical quality and patriotic appeal sealed his temporary fame and Mr. Noyes was everywhere praised prematurely as a great poet. Then, with the outbreak of war and the sudden flux of "new" poetry, his reputation suffered a gradual decline. His earlier work was not vital enough to last in the memory. There was too much beating of the big drum in the manner of—

Who are the Empire-builders? They
Whose desperate arrogance demands
A self-reflecting power to sway

A hundred little selfless lands?
Lord God of Battles, ere we bow
To these and to their soulless lust,
Let fall thy thunders on us now
And strike us equal to the dust.

The derivation here from Mr. Kipling's "Recessional" was all too obvious. Moreover, the spirit that seems to have inspired this kind of verse was considerably nulled by the great war. Mr. Noyes was never so much of a jingoist as Mr. Kipling, but in the pre-war years he allowed his verse to be over-influenced by topicalities, just as he tended to write poetry according to the popular conception of what poetry should be instead of according to the purer conception which is held in his various critical essays on the work of other poets. It may be—and who can wholly blame him for it?—that the constant chorus of praise with which he was surrounded persuaded him to write too easily, to forget the finer claims of his artistic conscience. In the light of his latest writings this suggestion can at least be entertained without offense.

In most of this earlier work there was too

much rhetoric in the composition of the poetry.
His ballads and many of his lyrics were padded
with fustian verse between their higher passages. And even in a poem as good as "Niobe"
there is a shade too much sound and fury.

How like the sky she bends above her child,
    One with the great horizon of her pain!
No sob from our low seas where woe runs wild,
    No weeping cloud, no momentary rain,
Can mar the heaven-high visage of her grief,
    That frozen anguish, proud, majestic, dumb.
She stoops in pity above the labouring earth,
    Knowing how fond, how brief
Is all its hope, past, present, and to come,
    She stoops in pity, and yearns to assuage its
        dearth.

This, and what follows, is, I feel, large utterance of an over-conscious order. There is a
sense of strain in "heaven-high visage," of dis-
comfort in the last line, and the whole, though
clearly enough said, is surely too elaborately
sung. Mr. Noyes has never been able to modify
his very genuine enthusiasm for big (not necessarily long) words. He loves a plangent line,

a ringing phrase. His favorite manner is the manner of "Our Fathers."

What Shadow is this up-towering through the night
Like a gaunt pine-tree on a mountain height
Round which the winds of God for ever flow?

and "The Lost Battle"—

It is not over yet—the fight
Where those immortal dreamers failed.
They stormed the citadels of night,
And the night praised them—and prevailed.
So long ago the cause was lost
We scarce distinguish friend from foe;
But—if the dead can help it most—
The armies of the dead will grow.

Mr. Noyes frequently strains too far to be noble.

It is not until his later work that he succeeds in combining the elements of poetry and rhetoric. His earlier poems are crowded with gratuitous roses, moons, galleons, and all the paraphernalia of the ready-made romantic manner. He drags in the picturesque word, the bright-coloured symbol without always stopping

204

to consider its fitness. A facile, though **not** really subtle metrist, he has usually been clever enough to dress such weaknesses in some kind of infectious rhythm.

Like many another English poet whose work reveals progressive improvement, Mr. Noyes appears to be known in America chiefly by this less satisfactory early work. His prolonged stay at Princeton University, to say nothing of his various lecture tours through the United States, sustained his American reputation during the years when the revival of interest in poetry began. But even in the United States his more recent writings do not appear to be very well known by comparison with such volumes as *The Flower of Old Japan, Lord of Misrule,* and *The Forty Singing Seamen.* That this should be so is an unhappy irony in view of the fact that only during the past six years has he really achieved a poetry which compels high admiration. It is early as yet to attempt any valid criticism of *The Torch Bearers,* the ambitious trilogy, epic in its character and proportions, of which the first two books only have been pub-

lished. The purpose of this enormous work,
in the poet's own words, is to follow "the great
moments of science, when, after long labour, the
pioneers saw their facts falling into significant
order." In the first book, "Watchers of the
Sky," Mr. Noyes is concerned with the history
of astronomy; in the second, "The Book of
Earth," he follows the discoveries of such men
as Pythagoras, Aristotle, Leonardo, and Goethe
in their struggles to solve the profound mys-
teries surrounding the origin and nature of man.
This very ambitious poem springs directly from
the author's genuine sense of wonder. I say
genuine because the verse in which his ideas are
conveyed rings true from the outset. Here is
all the difference between his old and new work.
This recent poem, which might so easily have
toppled into dullness, is actually his most exciting work. Many of its best passages are executed in something akin to the grand manner.
He looks down from the Sierra:

> Once, as we rounded one steep curve that made
> The head swim at the canyoned gulf below
> We saw through thirty miles of lucid air

Elvishly small, sharp as a crumpled petal
Blown from the stem, a yard away, a sail
Lazily drifting on the warm blue sea.

Mr. Noyes has always used his eyes to excellent
effect. He can excel in sweeping description.

I saw the green thread of the Colorado,
The dragon of rivers, dwarfed to a vein of jade.

Even better is the passage, also from "The Book
of Earth," beginning:

The tallest pine was but a feather
Under my feet in that ocean of violet gloom.
Then with a dizzying brain I saw below me
A little way out, a tiny shape, like a gnat
Flying and spinning, now like a gilded grain
Of dust in a shaft of light, now sharp and black
Over a bloodred sandstone precipice. "Look!"
The Indian guide thrust out a lean dark hand
That hid a hundred forests and pointed to it,
Muttering low "Big Eagle" . . .

The passage on the Grand Canyon will suffer
little in comparison with Shakespeare's description of Dover Cliff in *King Lear*.

This is a really fine achievement. At its side

—and there are other almost equally fine passages in *The Torch Bearers*—the great bulk of the poet's previous work pales into insignificance. In his earlier work the language usually exceeded the ideas. If Mr. Noyes finds his final balance in the forthcoming and final book of *The Torch Bearers* we may expect a really important contribution to the poetry of this decade, something far superior to anything he has yet written.

Nevertheless the balance of his achievement is still quantitatively on the wrong side. While we are to be grateful for such poetry as has just been quoted, it is impossible to forget that it is not common in the poet's collected work. For a time the barrel organ has changed into something more nearly resembling a real organ. It is impossible not to grant some real justification to the poets and critics in England who have refused to concede high honours to Mr. Noyes' verse when we consider it as a whole. To put the matter in a colloquial nutshell, he has failed in the dangerous attempt to eat his cake and have it too. He has not been able to create

an audience of poetry-lovers out of an audience
of verse-likers. He will not easily win the con-
fidence of those who recognized the comparative
coarseness of his previous work. On the other
hand, very few of the people who admired "The
Barrel Organ" (Come down to Kew in lilac-
time) will be likely to appreciate *The Torch
Bearers*, for it belongs to an altogether different
class of literature. It is not as though the difference were between, say, a good and a bad poem
by Wordsworth. There it would be the matter
of the absence or presence of a characteristic
ecstasy. The difference between these poems
by Mr. Noyes is between two planes of writing,
the one, poetry, the other, ordinary picturesque
verse, making a bid for the praise of the multitude. Mr. Noyes has not really deserved to be
treated as an important poet until quite recently.
In general his verse may be divided into one of
the two categories suggested above. They have
little to do with his subject-matter as such, or
even with his mood. Even his jingoism rises
at times into something akin to the best kind
of patriotism. But even in this strain he has

209

never succeeded half so well as his original,
Mr. Kipling, or that other excellent poet, Sir
Henry Newbolt. In his lyrical mood, again,
Mr. Noyes is too often the mere versifier. In
the world of poetry there is a fixed gulf between
such things as

> When Salomon sailed from Ophir . . .
> The clouds of Sussex thyme
> That crown the cliffs in mid-July
> Were all we needed—you and I—
> But Salomon sailed from Ophir,
>   And broken bits of rhyme
> Blew to us on the white chalk coast
> From O, what elfin clime?

and the genuine pulse of a more recent poem,
"Seagulls on the Serpentine":

Memory, out of the mist, in a long slow ripple
    Breaks, blindly, against the shore.
The mist has buried the town in its own oblivion.
    This, this is the sea once more.

Mist—mist—brown mist; but a sense in the air of
    snowflakes!
    I stand where the ripples die,

Lift up an arm and wait, till my lost ones know me,
Wheel overheard, and cry.

Salt in the eyes, and the seagulls, mewing and
swooping,
Snatching the bread from my hand;
Brushing my hand with their breasts, in swift ca-
resses
To show that they understand.

O why are you so afraid? We are all of us exiles!
Wheel back in your clamorous rings!
We have all of us lost the sea, and we all remember.
But you—have wings!

The second poem comes to us with that air
of authentic experience which only the poet who
is an artist in verse can communicate. It is
balanced, proportionate in language, rhythm,
rhyme, and feeling; its component parts are
welded in such a way as to disguise the welder's
art. But the first depends too much on the
fortuitous associations of the proper nouns; it
is only casually "stuck" together; it is loose,
verbose, superficially and unsatisfactorily con-

211

ceived and executed. The poet's technique is seldom so poor as we see it here. Mr. Noyes has never lacked facility in making verses. Facility may almost be said to have been his curse. Even at its best his verse is rather too uneconomical to rank with the very finest contemporary work. He multiplies words to gain effects that other living poets would achieve in half the space and with half the apparent energy. (Notice the "This, this" in the first stanza above.) It may be remarked as a slight but significant instance that he has always relied to a suspicious degree upon the extraneous aid of punctuation to emphasize his meaning and metre. The pauses in a good poem should be implicit. But Mr. Noyes is continually forced into the use of the dash in order to compel a pause in the verse at some place where the reader, lacking the dash, would not make a momentary halt. This may be observed in the last line of "Seagulls on the Serpentine." His repeated use, not only in this particular poem, of the mark of exclamation (thrice) further argues how, in the poet's own view, his verse does not carry its own vital emphasis by the sole means of the word and metre. Matthew Arnold has been blamed for his constant use of italics and expletive syllables like "Oh!" and "Ah!" for parallel purposes. The blame is justified. "Oh!" and "Ah!" and the mark of exclamation are the infallible signs of the inadequate versifier who cannot make his words do their own work. Thus when he means more than the words actually say he tries to stay the reader by one device or the other. This minor point is not irrelevant to present considerations. For the art of Mr. Noyes is seldom so skilful as to be able to dispense with these extraneous aids. They indicate better than anything else the shortcomings of his artistry. The first-class poet only uses such devices as a means to emphasize something already carefully emphasized in his words, and even then, with scrupulous economy. In most instances they will be superfluous. In the poetry of Mr. Noyes they are seldom superfluous, but some could be abandoned without any grave loss in the poem previously mentioned.

He works best on a large canvas. He is not a poet who can paint the streaks of the tulip, either literally or metaphorically. His effects at their best are of the bold and generous kind apparent in "Drake" and *The Torch Bearers*. He cannot command those delicate subtleties of sense and sound that mark so much of what is typical in the work of his best contemporaries. But it would be a great mistake to let this lack obscure his characteristic, and sometimes peculiar, virtues. There is something essentially big in many of his more meditative poems. Take the close of his recent sonnet, "On a Hospital":

Grave eyes will watch and hearts grow numb with
    pain,
Till the new hope that makes the eyes grow blind
Breathes, and the long suspense breaks down in
    tears
And quiet skill, content to serve its kind
Turns to new conflicts through uncounted years.

The truth is that underneath all his noisy optimism, melodrama and rhetoric (discounting for the moment those earlier jingles wherein he made a bid for immediate popularity) there exists a mind of large and generous quality, ever ready in sympathy, sensitive to the eternal struggle between man and his problems. When he touches upon the eternal verities—increasing age, death, love in its nobler aspect, the shackles often fall away and he becomes wholly free of the larger world of poetry. Thus, in "The Shadow," he addresses himself:

Day by day, in your eyes, the light grows dimmer,
  With the joy you have sung.
You knew it would go; but, ah, when you knew it
     and sang it
  Your heart was young.

And a year to you then was an age; but now, said
     the Shadow,
  Malignant and cold,
The light and the colour are fading, the ecstasy
     dying,
  It is time to grow old.

Oh, I could have borne the worst that he had to tell
     me,
  Lost youth, age, death;

But he turned to breathe on the quiet heart sleeping
    beside me
  The same cold breath.

And there by the throat I grappled him. "Let me
    bear all of it.
Let her dream on."
Soundlessly, shadow with shadow, we wrestled to-
    gether,
  Till the grey dawn.

This, obviously one of his most intimately personal utterances, reveals depths and a quality
of feeling which are too often absent in his
workaday writings. It is a pity that the one
false note, the physical image of "grappling"
in the last stanza should exist to mar an otherwise fine poem. That tiny hint of the melodramatic imagination which, in earlier pieces,
so often led him to exaggerate unduly, should
have found no place in "The Shadow."

Perhaps the greatest merit of Mr. Noyes's
work—and it cannot be too highly praised today
—is its simplicity and straightforwardness. If
anything he dots too many I's and crosses too
many T's. He means just what he says and

216

no more. Occasionally, unfortunately, he perhaps means even less than he appears to say. His verse, even when it deals, as in *The Torch Bearers*, with the very quality and range of the human intellect, can never be called intellectual. The reader cannot plunge through depth after depth of parallel meaning, as in the merely superficially simple poems of Mr. Yeats and Mr. de la Mare. In the strictest sense of the word Mr. Noyes is a simple poet—"elementary," or "obvious" might be better words if we could divorce them from certain uncomplimentary connotations. He is to be compared with Longfellow rather than with Wordsworth in this matter of simplicity. One does not return to his earlier poetry with the knowledge that each new reading will increase one's sense of its significance. Its values are face-values; its music, plain song, seldom harmonic. Only in the longer, later, more ambitious work is there a hint of a fuller purpose. In *The Torch Bearers* Mr. Noyes set out to conquer new latitudes of poetry. It will be interesting to see what treasure he ultimately brings home.

217

NICHOLAS VACHEL LINDSAY

Nicholas Vachel Lindsay

NICHOLAS VACHEL LINDSAY occupies
a curiously isolated position among modern
poets even in his own country. The character
of his work has been determined to an extreme
degree by the character of his environment and
at first sight there is something anachronistic
about his appearance in this century, chiefly because his poetry reflects the chaos and flux of
popular imagination in a country where races,
tongues, creeds, superstitions, cultures, are brew-
ing together as they have brewed nowhere else
in the world for hundreds of years. He is,
in fact, the most American of American poets.
The work of others, like Mr. Edwin Arlington
Robinson and Mr. Robert Frost, still mainly
reflects Anglo-Saxon America, and their artistic
consciences derive from English literature
through the Longfellow-Bryant-Whittier tradition. They owe only incidental debts to the
nature of their environment. One can well im-
agine Mr. Robinson, for instance, apart from
the United States. His work has few particu-

larly American characteristics: it reflects thoughts, feelings, scenes, which, in kind if not in colour, are common enough elsewhere. Even Mr. Frost, in spite of his distinctively American temperament, might have occurred in a different environment. The New England of his poetry, after all, is only another miniature, painted in his own phenomenally original colours, of the world in general, as he himself has insisted. It exists like a stage-setting—comparable to the Wessex of Thomas Hardy, or Mr. Housman's vaguer but no less microcosmic Shropshire—for the kind of action that belongs to no particular nation, place, or time. He can only be superficially regarded as "the interpreter of New England." Like Mr. Robinson he takes comparatively little from his environment which, in kind, is not equally available outside America.

But Mr. Lindsay is different. Much of his poetic "material" is peculiar to modern America and no man born and bred anywhere else could conceivably have written a body of poetry even

remotely resembling his.   Its very noise is
American.

I am the Kallyope, Kallyope, Kallyope,
Tooting hope, tooting hope, tooting hope, tooting
    hope;
Shaking window pane and door
With a crashing cosmic tune,
  With the war-cry of the spheres,
Rhythm of the roar of noon,
Rhythm of Niagara's roar,
  Voicing planet, star, and moon,
SHRIEKING of the better years.

And the same is true of its spirit and sense.
His poetry has been shaped to fit his immediate
audience in almost the reverse sense of Wordsworth's famous dictum that the poet creates the
taste by which he is enjoyed.   Again, poets like
Mr. Frost and Mr. Robinson have their coun-
terparts in other countries, men with something
of the same intellectual and emotional outlook.
In the last analysis they conform to some known
type.   But, apart from the fact that his work
has certain fundamental recognitions common

in all good poetry, Mr. Lindsay, in our own time, is virtually *sui generis.* In some respects, perhaps, he resembles those early makers of literature, the wandering minstrels and bards who, in Europe, first used the unwritten songs and legends of the folk as a point of departure for their own extemporizations. Even this resemblance is possibly more suggestive than true. True it is, however, that his work owes more than its mere surface manner to certain oral traditions that even print has not killed in some quarters of the United States. Moreover, his art has been less directly influenced than that of most modern poets by the written art of his predecessors. He is the only living poet who is not, primarily, a closet poet.

Like so many American authors, Mr. Lindsay has spent a large part of his time touring the United States, early in his career as a tramp "trading rhymes for bread," more recently as an established author trading recitals for cake, yet all the time preaching his personal beliefs in the spirit of a crusading missionary. But his poems, unlike those usually heard by modern

224

audiences, are obviously designed to appeal not
so much to the silent reader at the fireside as
to an audience of listeners crowded in a recital
hall.   In a word his work has a communal
character.   It is definitely written to be read
aloud, to be crooned, chanted, declaimed, and
even, on occasion, to be sung to some popular
song or hymn tune, like "Yankee Doodle"
("to be sung in a slower, more orotund fash-
ion"), "Gaily the Troubadour," or "The Blood
of the Lamb," as in "General William Booth
Enters Into Heaven."

*(Grand chorus of all instruments.   Tambourines to
the foreground.)*

The hosts were sandalled and their wings were fire!
(Are you washed in the blood of the Lamb?)
But their noise played havoc with the angel-choir.
(Are you washed in the blood of the Lamb?)
Oh, shout Salvation!   It was good to see
Kings and Princes by the Lamb set free,
The banjos rattled and the tambourines
Jing-jing-jingled in the hands of Queens.

(Reverently sung, no instruments.)
225

And when Booth halted by the curb for prayer
He saw his Master through the flag-filled air.
Christ came gently with a robe and crown
For Booth the soldier, while the throng knelt down.
He saw King Jesus, they were face to face,
And he knelt a-weeping in that holy place.
Are you washed in the blood of the Lamb?

Others, even more than this, require the co-operation of an excited audience to make their full effect, and many carry similar marginal notes concerning the manner of recitation.

Seen in cold print, many of these poems and "rhymed orations," as Mr. Lindsay sometimes calls them, are less impressive than when one hears them rendered by some gifted interpreter, preferably the poet himself, in the contagious atmosphere of a recital hall. The armchair reader is not much helped by a note to "The Kallyope Yell" stating that it should be given "in the peculiar whispered manner of the University of Kansas 'Jay Hawk Yell,'" nor will he be likely to attribute his lack of appreciation to his ignorance of that manner. And even those who have been fortunate enough to hear

Mr. Lindsay recite, when they read the same poems in his book, must admit a fatal loss of power in many instances. Pieces like "Daniel" and "The Kallyope Yell" cannot really be read; they must be heard. The poet with his fine voice and electric presence can abolish the distinction between rhetoric and poetry more often and more easily on the platform than on the printed page. He has succeeded in both places, but not always in the same poems.

Mr. Lindsay's is not a literary rhetoric like that, for example, which characterizes the earlier work of Mr. Alfred Noyes. It is a deliberate adaptation of negro pulpit oratory, especially the more histrionic oratory of the revivalist preachers. Moreover, his verse elaborately imitates the exotic rhythms and figures which are the most original features of the religious folk-song of the American negro. His poetry has been coloured throughout by the substance as well as the manner of these songs and sermons.

Andrew Jackson was eight foot tall.
His arm was a hickory limb and a maul.

227

His sword was so long he dragged it on the ground.
Each friend was an equal. Each foe was a hound.

This comprehends the bare formula which is so
much more powerfully elaborated elsewhere.
"How Samson Bore Away the Gates of Gaza"
is frank burlesque and, but for the rhymes, little more than a replica of the kind of thing it
imitates.

Once in a night as black as ink
She drove him out when he would not drink.

* * * * *

The air was black, like the smoke of a dragon,
Samson's heart was as big as a wagon.
He sang like a shining golden fountain.
He sweated up to the top of the mountain.
He threw down the gates with a noise like Judg-
    ment.
And the quails all ran with the big arousement.

But he wept—"I must not love tough queens,
And spend on them my hard-earned means.
I told that girl I would drink no more.
Therefore she drove me from her door. . . .

228

NICHOLAS VACHEL LINDSAY

(It is only a few weeks since I heard a negro
preacher begin his sermon with "Mr. and Mrs.
Prodigal had a son.") But in "John Brown"
the poet utterly transforms his model after the
first few lines, rising from

> I've been to Palestine.
> *What did you see in Palestine?*
> I saw the ark of Noah—
> It was made of pitch and pine.
> I saw old Father Noah
> Asleep beneath his vine.
> I saw Shem, Ham, and Japhet
> Standing in a line.
> I saw the tower of Babel
> In the gorgeous sunrise shine—
> By a weeping willow tree
> Beside the Dead Sea.

to the rhapsodical

> I've been to Palestine.
> *What did you see in Palestine?*
> Old John Brown.
> Old John Brown.
> And there he sits

229

To judge the world.
His hunting dogs
At his feet are curled.
His eyes half closed,
But John Brown sees
The ends of the earth,
The Day of Doom.
And his shot-gun lies
Across his knees—
Old John Brown,
Old John Brown.

And in "Simon Legree" (a negro sermon "to
be read in your own variety of negro dialect"
—so far does Mr. Lindsay insist on the voice) he
apotheosizes both the manner and substance of
his originals.

And the Devil said to Simon Legree:
"I like your style so wicked and free.
  Come sit and share my throne with me,
  And let us bark and revel."
And there they sit and gnash their teeth,
And each one wears a hop-vine wreath.
They are matching pennies and shooting craps,
They are playing poker and taking naps.

And old Legree is fat and fine:
He eats the fire, he drinks the wine—
Blood and burning turpentine—
Down, down with the Devil;
Down, down with the Devil;
Down, down with the Devil.

All Mr. Lindsay's work has been infected with this spirit. It is apparent in "The Congo" (where he is writing *about* the negro in an altogether broader manner), in his orations, and poems as different from one another as "Bryan" and "Hamlet." His habit of picturesque childish exaggeration, his love for pounding rhythms:

Then I heard the boom of the blood-lust song,
And a thigh-bone beating on a tin-pan gong.

—his characteristic simplicity, garish colour, and healthy coarseness all begin here.

He owes almost as great a debt to the parallel oratory of the whites, to the platform politicians, revivalists of the Billy Sunday type, and indeed to all lusty thumpers of the American tub. Their rhetoric, with all its violence, gusto, melodramatic quality, coarse irony, and florid

231

humour, culminates in Mr. Lindsay's poetry.
In "Roosevelt" we have a mere improvization
in the author's more casual manner, but even
his finest work has the same extemporaneous
air.

When the stuffed prophets quarrel, when the saw-
    dust comes out, I think of Roosevelt's gen-
    uine sins.
Once more my rash love for that cinnamon bear,
    Begins!
His sins were better than their sweetest goodness.
His blows were cleaner than their plainest kindness.
He saw more than they all, in his hours of black
    blindness
The hour of his pitiful spiritual fall
He was more of an angel than all of the host,
When with Lucifer's pride he gave up the ghost.

His yarns were nearer the sky than their truth.
His wildest tales in his fish-story hour
Nearer true than their truth.

Again, in his most recent but, unfortunately,
least impressive work, I understand that Mr.
Lindsay is attempting "new rhythms from the

primitive chants of the Indians." Their resemblance to the rhythms of everyday verse
and free-verse is so marked, however, that one
cannot regard them seriously side by side with
his debt to the negro.

> By Rising Wolf Peak
> There's a canyon of snow,
> Heart-shaped,
> Fair and white.
> It turns to blood-red
> If you climb there
> And stare
> Through the long night.

This is a typical specimen of the poet's recent
lapses which, unhappily, persist through three
volumes.

These various strains, then, recur throughout
Mr. Lindsay's verse and are admirably adapted
and mingled to serve its rhetorical purpose.
Out of these, chiefly, he has evolved a personal
idiom—style would hardly be a suitable word
—which recalls its antecedents at every turn,
in the coarse picturesqueness of its similes and

233

images, its blazing colour, its haste and gusto, frequently gaudy sentiment, and swollen simplicity. These are dangerous qualities; they encourage the mere noise and bombast into which Mr. Lindsay's poetry continually falls. But the texture of his best work displays them all.

And with the gipsies there will be a king
And a thousand desperadoes just his style,
With all their rags dyed in the blood of roses,
Splashed with the blood of angels, and of demons.
And he will boss them with an awful voice.
And with a red whip he will beat his wife.
He will be wicked on that sacred shore,
And rattle cruel spurs against the rocks,
And shake Calcutta's walls with circus bugles.
He will kill Brahmins there in Kali's name,
And please the thugs, and blood-drunk of the earth.
I know all this when gipsy fiddles cry.

And how admirably! Here, and in poems like "Bryan" and "The Congo," that idiom clothes the kind of substance that it can most effectively express. The poet is always at his best when writing about something in itself noisy, colour-

234

ful, vigorous, exciting, romantic, animated—
the McKinley-Bryan election, as seen at the
time through the eyes of a ten-year-old, a wild
negro jamboree, the breaking in of a colt, the
entry of a Salvation Army general into Heaven,
buffaloes stampeding, a tribal dance in central
Africa, or the passing and re-passing of the
thousand trains and automobiles on the Santa
Fé Trail—the noise of the traffic of a continent.
There is variety here as well as originality.
None of these themes are too full of noise for
Mr. Lindsay's voice: he translates their sounds
in the very syllables and rhythms that describe
their appearances.

Smokeblack freights on the double tracked railroad
Driven as though by the foul fiend's ox-goad,
Screaming to the West coast, screaming to the East,
Carry off a harvest, bring back a feast,
And harvesting machinery and harness for the beast.
The hand-cars whizz and rattle on the rails,
The sunlight flashes on the dinner-pails.

* * * * *

I brag and chant of Bryan, Bryan, Bryan,
Candidate for president who sketched a silver Zion,

The one American poet who could sing outdoors,
He brought in tides of wonder, of unprecedented
    splendor,
Wild roses from the plains, that made hearts tender,
All the funny circus silks
Of politics unfurled,
Bartlett pears of romance that were honey at the
    cores,
And torchlights down the streets to the end of the
    world.

*   *   *   *   *

Fat black bucks in a wine-barrel room,
Barrel-house kings with feet unstable,
Sagged and reeled and pounded on the table,
Pounded on the table,
Beat an empty barrel with the handle of a broom,
Hard as they were able,
Boom, Boom, BOOM,
With a silk umbrella and the handle of a broom
Boomlay, boomlay, boomlay, BOOM.
THEN I had religion, THEN I had a vision.
I could not turn from their revel in derision.
THEN I SAW THE CONGO, CREEPING
    THROUGH THE BLACK,

NICHOLAS VACHEL LINDSAY

CUTTING THROUGH THE FOREST WITH A
GOLDEN TRACK.

Then along that riverbank
A thousand miles
Tattoed cannibals danced in files.

And in all these poems we may remark a touch
of that naïvety and exaggeration which is more
nakedly apparent in his negro burlesques and
imitations.

Because of his characteristic stridency it is
all too easy to think of Mr. Lindsay as a noisy
enthusiast flaunting crimson banners and beating a big drum at the street-corners of literature.
Much of his work rings with the same sound
and fury as we have heard above, but, lacking
the same poetic excitement, degenerates into
the easiest kind of rhetoric, a kind of self-
parody in which the poet exaggerates all the
sensational elements of his art. It would be
ungenerous to dwell on such failures as "The
Fireman's Ball" with its disingenuous close, or
"Bob Taylor's Birthday" (". . . . of all my
productions the one least intended for cold

237

print. . . . I urge all my friends to amend it as they read it"). These are typical things in his more florid work that answer the groundlings' conception of poetry. But though Mr. Lindsay often rants too loudly, points too far, and even appears sometimes to play down to his audience, it must be remembered that he is the only living poet who has deliberately addressed himself, though, of course, not exclusively, to an unlettered audience. He is to modern poetry what the Salvation Army is to modern religion—a revivalist with thousands of converts to his credit.

This last comparison might be pressed further: for behind all this clamour and colour Mr. Lindsay appears in the rather unexpected character of prophet-preacher, the missionary of a peculiar sweetness and light. Throughout all his work, side by side with his patriotic fervour, the poet's social conscience makes itself powerfully if not always poetically felt. And although his very finest work can perhaps be appreciated for better reasons than this, its impulse, I think, takes much of its vitality from the same hopes and aspirations that are expressed in his rather prosaic apocalyptic poems. These are centred in the millennial future of America. Mr. Lindsay is a poet with a "message," one that is so particularly addressed to provincial America that it generally fails to transcend its immediate purpose and character. "This whole book," he says in the ramshackle preface to his Collected Poems, "is a weapon in a strenuous battlefield." He is fighting, of course, on the side of culture and sensitiveness against ignorance and apathy. "Each time I broke loose and went on the road in the Spring . . . it was definitely an act of protest against the United States commercial standard, a protest against the type of life set forth in *Babbitt* and *Main Street*." The reverberations of Mr. Lindsay's "three-times-loudly-proclaimed act of defiance" still sound in his "Gospel of Beauty" and through some kindred poems in which he prophesies and paints America's ultimate Golden Age. He is the William Morris of the Middle-West. He offers his apocalyptic visions with the air of one who has a compre-

239

hensive social gospel to preach. This, of course, is too good to be true.

The prototype of Mr. Lindsay's protest is Blake's

> I will not cease from mental fight,
> Nor shall my sword sleep in my hand,
> Till we have built Jerusalem
> In England's green and pleasant land.

But his American Jerusalem shines with all the conventional flowers, spires, and sunlight of the perennially Promised Land. Peace and joy abide there: statues fill the parks and incense the air: everything and everyone is blessed— until the poet creates misgivings by mentioning certain concrete details, the least alluring, perhaps, in his description of the ideal Tennessee.

> And our highest art will come in this Hereafter.
> And in all the parks so gay
> Sad young Shelleys, learning laughter,
> Amid high-school yells, and college-yells, and adventure yells,
> Weird Confederate yells, weird Union yells,

In scandalous music, whispered, hissing, drum-
    ming,
While above the skylark flying machines
Of all man's future humming.
Playthings of the fancy of young Shelleys that shall
    be,
And their little brothers and sisters . . .

In a much earlier poem Mr. Lindsay prophesies
for his own State.

> I saw wild domes and bowers
> And smoking incense towers
> And mad exotic flowers
> In Illinois.
> Where ragged ditches ran
> Now springs of Heaven began
> Celestial drink for man
> In Illinois.

And this is to be achieved "by laughter and by
prayer, by casting off all care in Illinois." The
fancy is less feeble though still crude in another prophecy of a time when

. . . on our old, old plains some muddy stream
Dark as the Ganges, shall, like that strange tide—

(Whispering mystery to half the earth)
Gather the praying millions to its side.
And flow past halls with statues in white stone
To saints unborn today, whose lives of grace
Shall make one shining universal church
Where all faiths kneel, as brothers, in one place.

But all this reads more like social propaganda
than the poetry of an artist who has had real
visions. The absurd climax is reached when
Mr. Lindsay replies to one "Impatient with
Visions and Utopias" with the vaguest of all his
visions, in which men are shown sowing flowers
instead of grief, laying precious pavements with
a song, and founding new shrines while "passion is turned to civic strength" (but how?) and
innocent children march singing in flowered
robes.

The same shallow, artificial idealism tends to
sap the strength of Mr. Lindsay's "Gospel of
Beauty" which, nevertheless, considered as a
social gospel for an American democracy, is
probably very sensible. The poet is a better
preacher than prophet. He looks back with
reverence and pride to the pioneers who

242

founded his native Middle West and resents all
that has happened since the trader followed
them from the East. He looks askance at the
big cities and suggests that the salvation of
American civilization lies in the little prairie
towns, sighing for

> the sweet life wrenched and torn
> By thundering commerce, fierce and bare.

He looks too at his own town, Springfield, and
utters a warning which, of course, nobody will
hear.

> Let not our little town be large, remembering
> That little Athens was the Muses' home,
> That Oxford rules the heart of London still,
> That Florence gave the Renaissance to Rome.

The rest comprehends an ambitious outline of
what must be done to make a city in whose parks
a student from afar would choose to starve
rather than go home: the *how* of the problem
is not mentioned. The fact that such an omis-
sion can occur to the reader reflects on the poetic
quality of Mr. Lindsay's gospel. It is sadly

doctrinaire. One prefers the poet in the
frankly defeated, unprophetic mood of "Why
I Voted the Socialist Ticket."

> I am unjust, but I can strive for justice.
> My life's unkind, but I can vote for kindness.
> I, the unlovely, say life should be lovely,
> I, that am blind, cry out against my blindness.
>
> Come, let us vote against our human nature,
> Crying to God in all the polling places . . .

This, though clumsy, is at least convincing. So,
too, is his lament for the multitude. . . .

> Not that they starve, but starve so dreamlessly,
> Not that they sow, but that they seldom reap,
> Not that they serve, but have no gods to serve,
> Not that they die, but that they die like sheep.

Mr. Lindsay is a poet whose implications always
point further than his explications. And even
his implications, when they are deliberately
made, as in "The Litany of the Heroes," that
colorful hotch-potch of lessons drawn from
the lives of famous men from Buddha to President Wilson, make doubtful poetry. He can-

not afford to adapt his manner to fit the didactic
mood. Even his characteristic rhetorical manner cannot be made to fit it except when, crown-
ing some argument, the poet falls back on the
spell-binding repetitions of the revivalists.

> The moral,
> The conclusion,
> The verdict now you know:—
> "The saloon must go,
> The saloon must go,
> The saloon,
> The saloon,
> The saloon,
> Must go. . . ."

And this, though it might be chanted to some
purpose at a mass meeting of sympathizers, is
utterly ineffective in print.

In the end it is neither as a preacher nor a
prophet that Mr. Lindsay achieves unchallenge-
able poetry although his transcendentalism occasionally appears dramatically transmuted in
his best work, as, for instance, in his justifiably

garish vision of the redemption of the negro
race at the end of "The Congo."

(*With growing deliberation and joy.*)

Then along that river, a thousand miles
The vine-snared trees fell down in files.
Pioneer angels cleared the way
For a Congo paradise, for babes at play,
For sacred capitals, for temples clean.
Gone were the skull-faced witch-men lean.
There, where the wild ghost-gods had wailed
A million boats of the angels sailed
With oars of silver and prows of blue

(*In a rather high key—as delicately as possible.*)

And silken pennants that the sun shone through.
'Twas a land transfigured, 'twas a new creation.
Oh, a singing wind swept the negro nation
And on through the backwoods clearing flew:—

*To the tune of "Hark, ten thousand harps and
voices."*

"Mumbo-Jumbo is dead in the jungle.
Never again will he hoo-doo you.
Never again will he hoo-doo you."

This is sheer rhapsody and, as such, rises to a
poetic plane which is never attained by the poet's
more carefully calculated apocalyptic pieces.
Again, by implication, in "Bryan" and some
other poems, where Mr. Lindsay laments the
defeat of his political and social hopes, not
overtly in his character as a preacher, but merely
as one of the defeated party, his plain emotions
reflect the terms of his gospel in glowing poetry.

> Election night at midnight:
> Boy Bryan's defeat.
> Defeat of Western silver.
> Defeat of the wheat.
> Victory of letterfiles.
> And plutocrats in miles
> With dollar signs upon their coats,
> Diamond watch-chains on their vests
> And spats on their feet.
> Victory of custodians,
> Plymouth Rock,
> And all that inbred landlord stock.
> Victory of the neat.
> Defeat of the aspen groves of Colorado valleys,
> The bluebells of the Rockies,

247

And blue bonnets of old Texas,
By the Pittsburgh alleys.
Defeat of alfalfa and the Mariposa lily.
Defeat of the Pacific and the long Mississippi.
Defeat of the young by the old and silly.
Defeat of tornadoes by the poison vats supreme.
Defeat of my boyhood, defeat of my dream.

For once, by forgetting his mission, Mr. Lindsay writes a poem to make the reader remember it.

But, in spite of all shortcomings, the poet's writings as a prophet and preacher are really attempts to subserve a vital poetic purpose which, taking his poetry all in all, Mr. Lindsay has admirably fulfilled. The original impulse of his work springs from a single realization whose seed is to be found in one of his earliest pieces, "Springfield Magical."

In this, the City of my Discontent,
Sometimes there comes a whisper from the grass,
"Romance, Romance—is here. No Hindu town
Is quite so strange. No citadel of Brass
By Sinbad found, held half such love and hate;

No picture-palace in a picture book
Such webs of Friendship, Beauty, Greed, and Fate."

"Wild legends, old and new, burn round my
bed," he says in another stanza. As poetry this
may be negligible: but the inherent realization
cannot be too strongly emphasized in justification of our description of Mr. Lindsay as "the
most American of American poets." It would
have been all too easy for the young Middle-
Westerner to persuade himself, like the heroes
of a thousand novels set in the central states,
that Romance (with the capital) might be found
anywhere in the world sooner than in Illinois.
But his mind was too tough for that. The
Mason and Dixon line ran through the house
in which he was born (it still runs through his
heart, he tells us): Lincoln himself had been
entertained there and his tomb stood almost at
the poet's door. "I was stuffed with family
history in my helpless infancy." There was a
Red Indian among his ancestors.

I am nearer her kin by far
Than the British who strut and boast

That they are the kin of William the Norman,
And his ravishing host.

His fathers came from Kentucky and he and
his sister "were still called rebels by the other
children in the schoolyard." In his infancy he
never heard of New England; but he heard of
Europe every day. This is enough to suggest
the beginnings of Mr. Lindsay's national feeling, or "patriotism" as we used to call it. He
is American to the core.

> We here renounce our Saxon blood.
> Tomorrow's hopes, an April flood
> Come roaring in. The newest race
> Is born of her resilient grace.
> We here renounce our Teuton pride:
> Our Norse and Slavic boasts have died:
> Italian dreams are swept away,
> And Celtic feuds are lost today. . . .
> She sings of lilacs, maples, wheat,
> Her own soil springs beneath her feet,
> Of springtime
> And Virginia
> Our Mother, Pocahontas.

250

This is the fundamentally reverential but rhapsodic spirit in which he approaches an America that has yielded him all the romance a poet could desire. He comes to poetry, on one hand, from the museums and libraries of the Middle West, bringing that superficial, encyclopaedic kind of culture, common in America, which smatters a man's mind with famous names and incidents, shreds and patches of fact and fiction from the history, literatures, arts, and mythologies of Europe and Asia. In all these matters his poetic equipment is unorganized, impressionistic, and slightly unreal. He can ask such a question as—

In the light of the maxims of Chesterfield, Mencius,
Wilson, Roosevelt, Tolstoy, Trotsky,
Franklin or Nietzsche, how great was Confucius?

which has neither the humour nor the point of a similar passage in "Kalamazoo"—

Why do the lean hyenas glare
Where the glory of Artemis had begun—
Of Atlanta, Joan of Arc,

251

Lorna Doone, Rosy O'Grady
And Orphant Annie all in one?

—and even that is rather silly. But, on the
other hand, Mr. Lindsay comes to poetry from
the forty-eight States, from the great cities, the
little prairie towns, the wheat belts, from the
Rockies and the Pacific, the villages of New
Mexico and New England. He has felt the
pulse of the American heart, identified himself
with its beat, worshipped at the shrines of his
country's great men from Washington to Wilson, and amplified the national legends, all in
a poetry that echoes to the rhythms and sounds
of the American language *as it is spoken*.

For these reasons the significance of his work
is considerably intensified when Mr. Lindsay
can be seen, as it were, against the American
horizon. A visit to the United States adds little
that is vital to an Englishman's previous appreciation of, say, "North of Boston" and even less
to his feeling for Mr. Robinson's fine work.
But, at first sight, Mr. Lindsay's references are
inevitably less comprehensible than theirs.

Happily, the loss of significance is not always accompanied by a poetic loss. In "Bryan" (perhaps his best single poem, though in some ways, the most allusive and localized of all) the loss actually results in a poetic gain. This poem is more admired in England, I believe, by people who do not understand a tenth of its political implications than in the United States where many readers can personally recall the presidential election of 1896. The rhapsody of names at the close, each name telling its own tale, is like the catalogue of heroes in an ancient epic. Indeed, the whole poem has a certain epic quality.

Where is McKinley, Mark Hanna's McKinley,
His slave, his echo, his suit of clothes?
Gone to join the shadows with the pomps of that
       time,
And the flame of that summer's prairie rose.

Where is Cleveland whom the Democratic platform
Read from the party in a glorious hour?
Gone to join the shadows with pitchfork Tillman,
And sledgehammer Altgeld who wrecked his power.

253

SOME MODERN POETS

Where is Hanna, Bulldog Hanna,
Low-browed Hanna who said: "Stand pat"?
Gone to his place with old Pierpont Morgan.
Gone somewhere with lean rat Platt.

Where is Roosevelt, the young dude cowboy,
Who hated Bryan, then aped his way?
Gone to join the shadows with mighty Cromwell
And tall King Saul, till the Judgment Day.

Where is Altgeld, brave as the truth,
Whose name the few still say with tears?
Gone to join the ironies with old John Brown,
Whose fame rings loud for a thousand years.

Where is that boy, that Heaven-born Bryan,
That Homer Bryan, who sang from the West?
Gone to join the shadows with Altgeld the Eagle,
Where the kings and the slaves and the trouba-
    dours rest.

This certainly gains on the English swings anything it may lose on the American roundabouts.
But substitute

Where is that boy, that heaven-born Asquith,
That Homer Asquith who sang from the West?

Gone to join the shadows with Gladstone the Eagle,
Where the kings, and the slaves, and the trouba-
dours rest.

This written, by Mr. Kipling, would make a more romantic appeal to a citizen of Manchester, Missouri, than to one of Manchester, Lancs. He would certainly take it more seriously. "Bryan" gains congruity when it is read by people who do not know, or even care to know, the facts about its Tillmans and Platts. It is a poem like so many of Mr. Lindsay's poems that will improve with the years. This is Mr. Lindsay's temporary penalty but ultimate reward for triumphing over such intractable contemporary material. The power to triumph so is the surest evidence of his genius.